W9-CEU-506

Today's World

The Superpowers

Roger James

B T BATSFORD LTD
LONDON

CONTENTS

ACKNOWLEDGMENTS

The Author and Publishers thank the following for the illustrations which appear in this book: The Associated Press Ltd, Pages 15, 38, 46, 47, 71; Camera Press Ltd, Pages 5, 12, 18, 28, 29, 39, 41, 56, 64, 65; Chronicle Publishing Co., Page 32; *Crocodile*, Moscow, Page 26; *Economist*, Pages 9, 61; *Frankfurter Allgemeine Zeitung*, Page 61; Keystone Press Agency Ltd, Pages 44, 55, 62; NATO, Page 33; Novosty Press Agency, Pages 37, 38, 49; Popperfoto, Pages 19, 21, 22, 24, 25, 35, 60, 68; *Pravda,* Page 43; US Air Force, Pages 16, 42, 63. The maps and figures were drawn by Chartwell Illustrators.

General Editor
Dr James L Henderson
Formerly at Institute of Education
University of London
and Chairman, World Education Fellowship

First printed 1978
Second impression 1984

© Roger James 1978
ISBN 0 7134 0081 1

Printed and bound in Great Britain by
Anchor Brendon Ltd, Tiptree, Essex
for the Publishers B T Batsford Ltd
4 Fitzhardinge Street, London W1H 0AH

THE NEW GOLIATHS

There are three giants in the world today. They are possessed of huge stature, vast strength, and the ability to instil great fear. Few of the giant nations of the past enjoyed the power of today's trio. The might and influence of these three giants, the United States of America, China, and the Soviet Union, are all too obvious. In an age of superlatives, of superstars and supertankers, when only the biggest seems impressive enough, these three rank as superpowers. Their strength and capabilities tower high above those of other nations, casting light or gloom across the lives of most people on our globe, as a flick of a television switch or a glance at a newspaper will demonstrate.

The term 'superpower' seems to have been coined by an American, William T.R. Fox, writing in 1944, at a time when the three giants of today were allies at war, fighting against what appeared to be the super-military strengths of Germany and Japan. Since that time the appeal, use, and aptness of the term 'superpower' has grown, as have the might and influence of the three giants themselves.

The development of such power is all the more striking when one considers that two generations ago all three were isolationist countries of only the second rank, having developed from the colonial frontiers of great western European powers which they now dwarf in strength, size, and importance. More ironic still is the fact that they in part control these older imperial powers through the most obvious demonstration of their superpower — their staggering armed might. Superpower is many things, but at root it is co-terminous with global political, economic, and military strength, based upon international power politics and the frightening possibility of a nuclear holocaust. In this sense superpower is close to absolute power.

Despite a relatively meteoric rise to their superpower status, the future potential of all three of these giants had often been accurately forecast. Nearly two hundred years ago another giant of his day, the Emperor Napoleon, warned that China was 'a sleeping giant . . . wake her and the world will tremble'. At roughly the same time Baron Melchior von Grimm was writing to the Empress Catherine II of Russia that

Two empires will share the advantages of civilisation, of the power of genius, of letters, of arts, of arms and industry: Russia on the eastern side and America . . . on the western side, and we peoples of the nucleus will be too degraded, too debased, to know otherwise than by a vague and stupid tradition what we have been.

This sentiment was echoed by the Frenchman Alexis de Tocqueville, who toured the United States in the 1840s and concluded at the end of Part One of his *Democracy in America* that

There are at the present time two great nations in the world, which started from different points, but seem to tend towards the same end. I allude to the Russians and the Americans. Both of them have grown up unnoticed; and whilst the attention of mankind was directed elsewhere, they have suddenly placed themselves in the front rank among the nations, and the world learned of their existence and their greatness at almost the same time.
All other nations seem to have nearly reached their natural limits, and they have only to maintain their power; but these are still in the act of growth. All the others have stopped, or continue to advance with extreme difficulty; these alone are proceeding with ease and celerity along a path to which no limit can be perceived. . . . Their starting point is different, and their courses are not the same; yet each of them seems marked out by the will of Heaven to sway the destinies of half the globe.

In 1883, Sir John Seeley claimed that Russia and the United States were already 'enormous political aggregations' which would one day 'completely dwarf such European states as France and Germany and depress them into a

China ■ USA ☰ USSR ▒

Map of the World to show the positions of the three superpowers.

second class'. The warnings and expectations of these commentators were realized, so that on 4 August 1957 the *Sunday Times* declared: 'Ultimate power is concentrated today in the hands of two giants, the USA and the USSR. If they monopolise it, the ultimate decisions rest with them alone.' Twenty years later a third giant, one that had been sleeping, and has awakened, has joined the ranks of the superpowers, and Napoleon's prophecy may yet be true.

What, then, are these modern giants, these superpowers? How do they stand above other nations and differ from other powers? Wherein lie the contrasts between them and the old imperial powers like Rome and Britain? What are the bases of their power and how do they use it? In what ways do they affect our lives and dominate the world today?

Writing in 1956 Nathaniel Peffer sought to highlight the sources of a nation's power: 'What

constitutes power in our time? Clearly it is constituted of population, resources, accumulated wealth, industrial structure, scientific knowledge, and technological advancement.' You can, of course, say that these equal military might. Dean Acheson wrote that power has an economic base but a military form. No material or moral advantage is of any real consequence unless it has substance, the sanction of force, to back it up.

The Assyrian Empire was able to challenge and topple the neighbouring regimes mainly because its warriors possessed superior chariots and weapons of iron. Rome was expanded into an empire by meticulous military training and tactics. The Ottoman Turks burst to power and empire by the inclusion of military conquest as part of a religious creed. The British Empire, for all its industrial wealth, would not have been as far-flung and long-lived had it not enjoyed naval supremacy and the technological inferiority of its victims in military matters. Germany and Japan similarly used feats of arms to achieve staggering successes in the initial stages of the Second World War.

The fact that they failed and were ultimately defeated shows how vulnerable mere military might can be if not supported by the other sources of power Peffer highlighted. Since the downfall of Germany and Japan the three new giants, the United States, the Soviet Union, and, latterly, China, have commandeered a preponderance of power.

Indeed, for all their extensive resources of population, raw materials, scientific and technological knowledge, the most awe-inspiring aspect of superpower in the world today is the vast accumulation of nuclear and non-nuclear weapons and forces as well as the means with which to develop and use them. This huge military potential resulted in what Sir Winston Churchill chillingly described as 'a balance of terror'. After 1945 the world was for all intents and purposes divided between two monolithic power blocs, between the influences of capitalist America and communist Russia. This dual control of world affairs has now developed into a system of triple control, with an uneasy triangular relationship between the three superpowers.

The Tanzam Railway. Chinese engineers supervise African workers laying down a section of the 18 000-km railway which links the port of Dar es Salaam in Tanzania with the copper mines of Zambia. Built with an interest-free loan from China, the railway was opened in 1975 and has won China great esteem among Third World countries.

'Painting the globe red'. The territorial extent of the British Empire in 1897 can be clearly seen from this map.

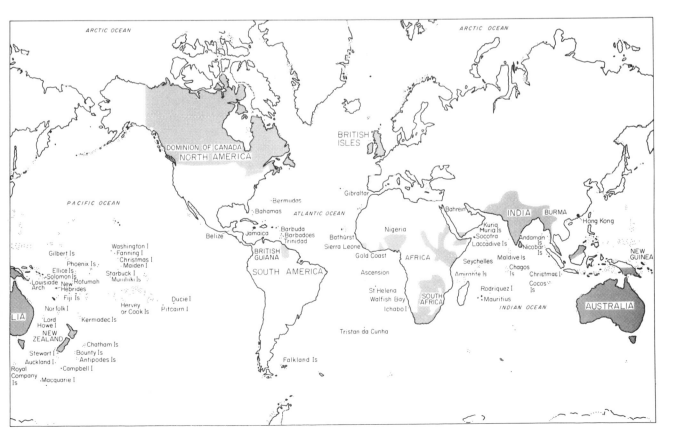

Military, economic, and political influence can now be exercised over immense spheres of interest. Each of the superpowers has a capacity to deploy the various elements of their power anywhere in the world where they consider their interests can be furthered or endangered. Thus one can find Chinese engineers building a railway in East Africa, American troops stationed in West Berlin, and Russians constructing deep-sea harbours in Cuba. One calls to mind the original definition of a superpower offered by William T.R. Fox in 1944: 'A power, whose armed force is so mobile that it can be deployed in any strategic theatre, as opposed to a great power, whose interests and influence are confined to a single regional theatre.' Thus, at the very time that the old colonial powers such as Britain and France were pulling back their military presence from overseas stations such as Indo-China and West Africa, American advisers and Russian technicians were being posted to Vietnam and Egypt. After the Second World War the old powers had neither the resources nor the will to attempt to continue their global roles. The superpower game was to be of a different stature and was to be played for massive stakes.

Superpower today is far more complex and penetrating than it was in the days of the European balance of power and the imperial adventures of its competitors in colonial areas. Fox was writing at the time of the transition of power, and superpower has even changed since then. He was writing at a time when air flight and rocketry were in their infancy, before the massive revolutions in communications and technology which have so shrunk the world. In defining the areas of superpower control one cannot neatly draw an outline on a map as one could outline the Mediterranean world of the Roman Empire, nor can one colour large tracts of land on a map an appropriate shade as one could to show the extent of the nineteenth-century British Empire. Superpower strength and influence are both invisible and global in extent. Apart from the satellite nations of Eastern Europe, overrun or 'liberated' by the Red Army in the 1940s, there are no clear territorial empires belonging to the superpowers. Even so, superpower knows no frontiers.

Outright military invasion or occupation (except as a last resort) is no longer feasible in the era of modern nationalism, countervailing Soviet power and potential domestic opposition, the argument runs, so neo-imperialism has developed new, more subtle methods. Through its vast economic power − the billions of dollars invested in the Third World by American-controlled multinational corporations; United States government control of economic assistance to under-developed countries, either directly in its bilateral programmes or indirectly through its domination of the major international financial institutions; the dependence of Third World countries on American markets for their exports of raw materials and commodities and imports of manufactured goods and modern technology; the centrality of the dollar in the world monetary market, etc. − the United States works to keep the rest of the world conservative, capitalist, and docile . . . .

In any case, economic power is supplemented by close American ties with conservative local elites, whose own continued status and power is dependent on United States support − the politicians; the bureaucrats; and especially the forces of repression, the military and the police, who are trained, financed, equipped and frequently led by American 'advisers'. At a more subtle and insidious level, there is the power of 'cultural imperialism', the cultural role of the United States in the world communications network and mass media, which provides the means to shape images and aspirations in ways consistent with the maintenance of world capitalism and United States domination.

If more forceful action is necessary to prevent undesirable change or shore up cooperative client governments, the argument runs, the CIA is always available to provide information, advice, propaganda, subsidies, bribes, weapons, private armies, and a whole repertoire of 'dirty tricks', including coups d'état and/or the murder of particularly stubborn recalcitrants. And if all else fails, direct military action, facilitated by the worldwide network of US bases and troop deployments, can shore up the empire at its weakest points, as in Lebanon, the Dominican Republic and Indo-China. (Jerome Slater 'Is United States Foreign Policy "Imperialist" or "Imperial"?' *Political Science Quarterly*, vol. 91, no. 1, spring 1976)

In this description of the radical, neo-Marxist view of American foreign policy Professor Slater was playing devil's advocate. But one could equally justify superpower activities as furthering mutual benefits and mutual security with the Third World. A blunt, but less detailed claim for global superpower involvement by the Soviet Union was made by Mr Gromyko, the Russian Foreign Secretary, to the Supreme Soviet in June 1968:

The Soviet Union is a great power situated on two continents, Europe and Asia, but the range of the country's international interests is not determined by its geographical position alone.... The Soviet people do not plead with anyone to be allowed to have their say in the solution of any question involving the maintenance of international peace, concerning the freedom and the independence of the people's and our country's extensive interests. This is our right, due to the Soviet Union as a great power. During any acute situation, however far away it appears from our country, the Soviet Union's reaction is expected in all capitals of the world. (Quoted in G. Urban (ed.) *Détente*, Universe Books, 1976)

China, one quarter of mankind, and the newest superpower, appears to be the most reluctant. Fitted by all definitions such as population, resources, and global activity to superpower status, she finds it more useful to deny such a role and to criticize the other two superpowers, reserving for herself a position at the head of the developing countries of the Third World.

China constantly launches attacks against what she claims are the other superpowers' monopolization and manipulation of power. At the United Nations Conference on Trade and Development in Kenya in May 1976, Chou Hua-min, the leader of the Chinese delegation, delivered a violent onslaught against the United States and the Soviet Union. Of the 153 conference members, 122 were representing the developing countries, and they appreciated the criticism of the two superpowers which China classifies as enemies of the Third World.

One superpower desperately clings to the old order and opposes the establishment of a new international order in order to preserve its vested interests. It endlessly preaches 'interdependence' and alleges that global prosperity rests on its leadership. To put it bluntly, it means nothing but to maintain the control, plunder and exploitation against developing countries .... The other superpower which is 'socialist' in name but socio-imperialist in essence, goes all out for treacherous acts to undermine the just struggle of the Third World while pretending to be in favour of a new economic order. (*Newsday*, 5 May 1976)

The Commonwealth Secretary-General, Mr Shridath Ramphal, has attacked the two superpowers for launching a new arms race that is directly destroying the prospects for an economic recovery, North and South alike ... 'The rules of international law are being made subservient to superpower paranoia and national machismo ... this obscene expenditure amounts, conservatively, to more than 1 million dollars spent for military purposes every minute of 1981.' ... There was a correlation between the increase in military spending and the downward slide in funds for aid and development. Taking the $650 billion spent on arms in 1981, which grew to $880 billion last year, he said that one minute's worth of this sum would feed 2,000 under-nourished children in a poor country for a year. 'The arms race now constitutes in itself a substantial obstacle to economic growth in developed and developing countries alike ... both the superpowers still refuse to acknowledge it.' (*The Guardian*, 22 November 1983)

From such claims one might deduce that superpower status is as much ideological and economic as military. However, the stark realities of world power today lie in the maintenance of huge armed man-power and the possession of sophisticated weapons of incalculable destructive force. In recent years the important events in international affairs have tended to occur where any two or all three of the superpowers have been concerned. In such areas smooth relations and stable conditions have proven difficult. The atmosphere has been tense and the mood one of confrontation. Stress areas have particularly persisted in the Middle East, where the United States and the Soviet Union both have client states; in Europe, where there has been a face-to-face stalemate of NATO and Warsaw Pact forces; and at various points around the ring of American forces and bases which have contained China since 1949. The superpowers have the world as their arena but only themselves to control the conflict.

THE CRITICAL IMAGE

The impact of the superpowers reaches far beyond their own national frontiers and the lives of their own peoples. The security, prosperity, and even the life-styles of their neighbours, allies, client states and satellites depend heavily upon them. The superpowers will usually deny any involvement in or control of any foreign country's affairs, but in fact exercise their power and influence in a variety of subtle ways. They each claim to be and are seen to be the leader of a bloc of states. Their actions are looked to for a lead and their reactions are regarded as a touchstone. They can create opinion and decide issues. Each of them realizes its power and relishes its use. This power allows them to act as champions and puppeteers; their use of it can establish them as saints or sinners, with little in the nature of restraint either way. Dr Henry Kissinger, the US Secretary of State, was fond of alluding to the need for the superpowers to exercise mutual restraint and come to understandings since there was no other capable sanction. Mr Callaghan, the British Prime Minister, made the same point at a meeting of international socialist leaders, when he warned the Soviet Union against deep involvement in African affairs: 'I am not denying the Soviet Union her legitimate rights as a superpower. But superpower status brings with it superpower responsibility — to know when to stay out' (*The Times*, London, 18 April 1977).

Each of the superpowers has experienced the criticism of its own citizens for exceeding its 'superpower rights' and ignoring its 'superpower responsibility'. This public dissent is perhaps more evident in the United States than in the closed societies of the Soviet Union or China, but it exists in all three superpowers to varying degrees of vociferousness and effect. In 1976 Arnosht Kolman, an 84-year-old member of the Soviet Academy of Sciences, a respected Marxist philosopher and early revolutionary follower of Lenin, spoke out in an open letter to Mr Brezhnev, the General Secretary of the Soviet Communist Party. Criticizing the superpower activities of the Soviet Union, he returned his Communist Party card of 58 years' standing, and requested political asylum in Sweden:

When your tanks and armies occupied Czechoslovakia submitting it to your political diktat and merciless economic exploitation — in short turning it into your colony — I lost any illusions I may have had about the nature of your regime . . . .

While preaching about 'international detente' and 'peaceful coexistence', the Soviet Union is, in fact, amassing at an increasingly fast rate nuclear weapons and rockets, is preparing new generations of mass destruction weapons and is preparing for aggressive wars.

It keeps vast armies outside its frontiers, builds more and more military bases in Europe, Asia and Africa, and is preparing for the occupations of Roumania and Yugoslavia. Under the guise of 'selfless aid' to the national liberation movements and developing countries, the Soviet Union is carrying out ceaseless attempts to infiltrate their ranks and establish its military and political overlordship in various corners of the earth; it is also supplying arms and providing support for most reactionary regimes and international terrorists.

This was a heart-felt cry from a loyal citizen who grew to hate the power he had helped to create. Examples of such dissatisfaction can be found in each of the superpowers, with military influences particularly criticized.

In 1961 President Eisenhower's 'Farewell Message' warned of the dangers he saw, even as a military man himself, in the power of what he termed 'the military-industrial complex':

We have been compelled to create a permanent armaments industry of vast proportions . . . . Now this conjunction of an immense military establishment and a large arms industry is new in the American experience. The total influence — economic, political, even spiritual — is felt in every city, every state house, every office of the Federal

"YOU MEN REALIZE THAT WE'RE IN A STRUGGLE TO PRESERVE OUR ENTIRE STANDARD OF SPENDING"

PENTAGON

ARMS CONTRACTORS

ARMED SERVICES COMMITTEE MEMBERS

ADMINISTRATION PLANS FOR ARMS CONTROL NEGOTIATIONS

©1977 HERBLOCK

Arms spending. A cartoon in the *Economist*, 19 February 1977.

military may seek and obtain over-mighty power is shown by this left-wing manifesto exhibited in Hunan in China in 1968:

Since the capitalist-roaders hold power in the army, some elements in it have not only discarded their flesh-and-blood relations with the people, but have even become tools for suppressing revolution. If, therefore, the Great Proletarian Cultural Revolution is to succeed, a radical change in the army is called for. The fact is that in the same year that Chairman Mao issued the order for the armed forces to live in their barracks they became divorced from the masses . . . . Local wars of various sizes, in which the army was sometimes directly involved, erupted in the country . . . . For a short time the cities were in a state of 'armed mass dictatorship' . . . . But the proclamation of the 5th September Directive (ordering the rebels to return their weapons) completely nullified Chairman Mao's rousing call to 'Arm the Left'. The working class was disarmed. The bureaucrats again came to power. (Quoted in John Gittings, *A Chinese View of China*, London, BBC Publications, 1973)

These expressions of citizen unrest with the strength and role of their countries all contain indications of the political and military might of the superpowers at home. Their might is even more clearly demonstrated abroad, when exercised upon other nations. Unimpeded direct action by the superpowers was seen with the Soviet Union in Hungary in 1956, Czechoslovakia in 1968, Afghanistan in 1979 and Poland in 1980, with China in Tibet in 1959, and with the United States in Vietnam after 1965 and in Grenada in 1983. When attempted by lesser powers, such as Britain, France and Israel during the Suez Crisis of 1956, or India and Pakistan in 1971, or Greece and Turkey over Cyprus in 1974, such direct action is snuffed out or pressurized by the superpowers, sometimes acting in collusion. British action in the Falklands in 1982 was an exception but was very closely monitored by both the United States and the Soviet Union.

Government. We recognise the imperative need for this development. Yet we must not fail to comprehend its grave implications. Our toil, resources and livelihood are all involved; so is the very structure of our society.

In the councils of government, we must guard against the acquisition of unwarranted influence, whether sought or unsought, by the military-industrial complex. The potential for the disastrous rise of misplaced power exists and will exist.

We must never let the weight of this combination endanger our liberties or democratic processes. We should take nothing for granted. Only an alert and knowledgeable citizenry can compel the proper meshing of the huge industrial and military machinery of defense with our peaceful methods and goals, so that security and liberty may prosper together. (Dwight D. Eisenhower, *Waging Peace*, Doubleday, 1966)

Similar fears that in a superpower state the

SUPERPOWER MUSCLE

Population

China	1,008,175,288
USA	231,960,000
USSR	271,203,000

(*UN Demographic Yearbook*, 1983)

Land area

China	9.6	(millions) sq. km.	3.7	(millions) sq. miles
USA	9.4	(millions) sq. km.	3.6	(millions) sq. miles
USSR	22.4	(millions) sq. km.	8.6	(millions) sq. miles

(*Observer Atlas of World Affairs*, 1971)

Gross National Product

	US$ per capita	% for defence	% growth per year
China	290	10.0	4
USA	11,360	6.1	3
USSR	4,550	14.0	4
UK	7,920	5.4	3

(*Whitaker's Almanack*, 1984)

Economic aid to foreign countries, 1975

China	2132?	(millions) US dollars	0.1	% of GNP
USA	4908	(millions) US dollars	0.3	% of GNP
USSR	1264	(millions) US dollars	0.05	% of GNP
UN request	—		0.7	% of GNP

(*New York Times*, 20 August 1976)

Armed forces personnel

	Total (millions)	Army (millions)	Navy (millions)	Airforce (millions)
China	3.94	3.15	0.3	0.49
USA	2.12	0.99	0.55	0.58
USSR	3.14	1.82	0.45	0.87

(*The Statesman's Yearbook*, 1983)

THE BALANCE OF TERROR

The ultimate power of the superpowers lies with their armed forces and their weapons of mass destruction. They possess such a devastating array of weapons and missiles carrying nuclear warheads, many already aimed and primed for launching at the push of a button, that civilized life would be threatened if any single one was fired. During the 1960s films like *Dr Strangelove* and *Failsafe* showed how delicate and dangerous the nuclear balance is. A mistake, an electronic fault, a madman or a misinterpretation of another superpower's actions could each begin a deadly sequence of events. Bertrand Russell, the philosopher, when asked what the weapons of the Third World War would be, declined to say, but added that the weapons of the Fourth World War would have to be rocks. William Greider wrote in the *Guardian* (15 March 1977):

To put the matter crudely, the atomic bomb dropped on Hiroshima represented by various estimates 13 000 to 20 000 tons of explosive. Now, according to one estimate, the United States has warheads aimed at Russia equivalent to 4 200 000 000 tons. A substantial portion of these are on submarines and are invulnerable to Russian attack. Thus, if Russia fired first today and wiped out America's land-based missiles, President Carter could still retaliate by wiping out all but the smallest towns − killing 20 million or 40 million or 100 million Russians, depending on how he chose the targets.

Yet for the same reasons Russia has essentially the same insurance policy. Its nuclear warheads, fewer but heavier, could strike back at America with comparable destructive force. It is this now familiar state of affairs which the global thinkers call mutually assured destruction; MAD for short: the doctrine which has kept both sides from shooting first.

The scale and terminology of the nuclear balance are equally difficult to understand. One cannot envisage 20, 40 or 100 million people dying or suffering terrible injury. One cannot picture a burnt and ruined world. Equally terms like 'megatonnage', 'throw-weight', 'first strike', 'missile gap', and 'overkill' sound almost clinically and mathematically innocent. Yet they are terms in a numbers game with potentially catastrophic implications.

A major nuclear war exploding 10 000 megatons, or about one-third of the world's atomic armoury, would not wipe out mankind, according to a new, highly technical report by the National Academy of Sciences. Nor would the radioactive fall-out be as harmful or pervasive as has long been feared. Apart from a few 'hot-spots' the effects of radioactivity would be limited in time (two-thirds of the fall-out occurring in the first year) and restricted in distance. An almost full recovery from nuclear radiation could be expected within 25 years; even less in the southern hemisphere.

Heartened? Don't be. A war on this scale, the report concludes, would destroy the stratospheric layer of ozone that filters off many of the earth's harmful ultra-violet rays. Up to 70% of the ozone in the northern hemisphere could be eliminated in such a war (by forming oxides with the nitrogen loosed by the bombs) and this would lead to unforeseen effects. An intelligent guess would include among these: disease epidemics among crops and farm animals on a global scale; an upset in the ecology of the oceans that would devastate the world's fish catch; and widespread suffering from skin cancer. Lack of ozone, not radiation, is now thought to be the disastrous side-effect of nuclear war . . . .

In a veiled reference to China the report suggests that a 'distant, populous other nation' might find the side-effects which it would suffer from a nuclear war between America and Russia would be 'acceptable', a nation that . . . implies that the concept of nuclear war is itself acceptable as a political decision. . . . The agency's report calculated that a 100-megaton attack on the United States would instantly kill 20% of the population. A 100-megaton attack would kill not fewer than 100 million people within the first few seconds (a nuclear explosion releases 90% of its energy in the first millionth of a second), without counting the deaths caused by radiation, cancer, disease and genetic change. After that, how many would be left to struggle with the problems of ozone loss? (*The Economist*, 18 October 1975)

Despite the horrors of this possibility, the United States now has about 9 500 warheads

The ultimate power. After this explosion at Nagasaki on 9 August 1945, the second atomic strike in three days, Japan finally surrendered to the United States.

and Russia around 7 500 (this figure has almost doubled in five years). China is estimated to possess 2 000-3 000 nuclear warheads. This huge arsenal is aimed at no more than a few hundred targets; in nuclear jargon there seems to be a massive 'overkill' potential. However, some missiles might fail to launch, or might be shot down, and whereas 50% of America's population is concentrated in three major areas, Russian and Chinese targets are more diffuse.

In an effort to maintain a balance of arms the superpowers seem to be locked in a technological struggle, trapped in an arms race with little logic but its own momentum. Research and development have taken over. Ever-increasing sums are spent on launching and delivery systems, antisubmarine warfare, laser beams, miniaturization, computer-guidance, and the like. It has taken only 30 years for technology to develop from the ungainly B29 bomber which dropped the atom bombs on Japan to the sophisticated wizardry of MX Peacekeeper. In the headlong race to be ahead, technology appears uncontrollable. Some new idea or technique emerges to alter the strategic balance.

Disarmament has never been successful, even before the era of mutually assured destruction. However, the realization by the United States and the Soviet Union of the dangers they were multiplying did result in a measure of mutual restraint and security. This realization became known as 'détente' and the Strategic Arms Limitation Talks (SALT) are perhaps the best example of it. Apart from the Limited Nuclear Test Ban Treaty of 1963 and the treaty on the non-proliferation of nuclear weapons of 1968, real agreements and understandings on the nuclear balance had been few. Following discussions begun in 1968, SALT 1 was signed by the United States and the Soviet Union in May 1972. This agreement virtually banned missile defence systems (ABMs) and established a four-year interim agreement on offensive missiles. Both the USA and USSR agreed to maintain only two ABMs, each with 100 interceptor missiles (a subsequent agreement reduced this to one ABM in July 1974). The USA was to maintain 1054 land-based missiles and 656 submarine-launched missiles, while Russia was to maintain 1618 and 950, respectively. In addition, the United States was to maintain 490 strategic bombers against Russia's 140. In November 1974 a summit meeting between the two superpowers resulted in the Vladivostok Agreement, which set a common ceiling on delivery systems. Both superpowers were to possess 2400 long range missile launchers and bombers, of which 1320 could be fitted with multiple independently targeted re-entry vehicles (MIRVs). Such agreements have demanded negotiating skills and technical knowledge of a high order — neither side is willing to concede too much or run the risk of misunderstandings in the final treaties. It took 200 meetings for the two superpowers to agree to a mutual ban on underground nuclear tests of over 150 kilotons in May 1976 to complement the 1974 mutual ban on underground nuclear weapons testing of the same size. Both sides realized the need for further agreements, but SALT 2 was not ratified by the American Senate because of the Russian invasion of Afghanistan. Despite this President Carter continued to declare that his ultimate aim was 'the elimination of all nuclear weapons from this earth'.

It is unlikely that this laudable ideal would ever be realized or allowed by the superpowers. The dangers of strategic or military inferiority, acquisition by smaller powers or terrorist groups, and mutual distrust are likely to maintain a nuclear potential with each superpower until new technology presents them with an alternative deterrent. Indeed, each of the agreements reached during the present decade has had far less substance than coverage in the media would suggest. Since SALT 1 the United States has doubled its primed arsenal of nuclear warheads and Russia has increased the number of its missiles to the limits of the agreement, accompanied by 15 complaints from the USA that SALT 1's terms have been broken. Much of the detail in the agreement left itself open to different interpretations by each side. The question of verification, of how each side monitors the other's observance of the agreement, is unsatisfactory.

Far from limiting arms, since SALT 1 Russia has deployed four new strategic delivery systems and is working on another ten. The United States is developing three. Technology has improved the accuracy, size, and mobility of delivery systems. No decisions or agreements have been reached regarding the awkward problems posed by missiles and bombers not included in the talks, such as the American 'Cruise' missile and the Russian 'Backfire' bomber. These are important delivery systems which could alter the whole nuclear balance.

Equally the bans on underground testing mean little in practice. That on weapons had no provision for verification or inspection. It was seen as a major concession when the Russians agreed to on-site inspection during tests for peaceful purposes. The very size of the explosions, 150 kilotons, is in fact seven times that at Hiroshima, and is hardly a 'limit'. Neither of the two superpowers actually uses such large blasts. The United States decided to discontinue them in 1973, although Russia sometimes has a use for them in such projects as river diversion and permafrost excavations for minerals and energy sources. Despite such limitations, the agreements which have been finalized have served a purpose in the general pursuit of détente and superpower restraint.

Both the United States and the Soviet Union have realized that they are in fact bound together in what has been termed an 'adversary partnership'. Nuclear weapons on the vast scale deployed by the superpowers are too destructive, they assure mutual ruin and annihilation. At such a level nuclear weapons almost cease to possess any political value. Dr Henry Kissinger made this point on 3 July 1974 when he exclaimed: 'One of the questions we have to ask ourselves as a country is what, in the name of God, is strategic superiority? What is the significance of it, politically, militarily, operationally, at these levels of numbers? What do you do with it?' (Quoted in Theodore Draper, 'Appeasement and Détente', *Commentary*, vol. 61, no. 2, February 1976)

President Carter warned in his Farewell Address of the growing threat of a nuclear war in which 'more destructive power than in the entire 1939-45 war would be unleashed every second for the long afternoon it would take for all the bombs and missiles to fall.' In the Second World War 3MT of high explosives were detonated. Today the superpowers possess 7,368MT, or 2,500 times the total used then. As Churchill said, such an amount of destructive power would serve only to make the rubble bounce.

Until the early 1970's, no one in the world questioned that the United States was the most powerful nation in the world. The existence of this U.S. power deterred overt aggression and forced the Communists to go under borders rather than over them.

The United States was able, because of this superiority, to deter Soviet intervention in the Berlin Crisis of 1948-49, the Middle East War in 1956 and in the Lebanon in 1958 when local U.S. naval superiority also played a critical role. In the Cuban missile crisis of 1962 a 15 to 1 U.S. advantage over the Soviet Union in nuclear weapons enabled Kennedy to face down Khrushchev. In 1973, when we ordered a world-wide alert to keep Soviet forces out of the Middle East during the Yom Kippur War, the United States and the Soviet Union were approximately equal in both strategic nuclear capability and theatre nuclear capability. The situation has changed drastically since then.

For a quarter of a century, American nuclear superiority kept the peace. Now that superiority is gone, and if present trends continue the Soviets will have strategic nuclear superiority by the mid-1980's. What is superiority? In our hands it was the safety margin that ensured that the Soviets would not risk a nuclear exchange in their pursuit of their goal of world domination. In Soviet hands it becomes the margin that enables them to proceed with local aggression without expecting a massive nuclear response. (Richard Nixon: *The Real War,* Sidgwick & Jackson, 1980)

SINEWS OF SUPERPOWER

The B1 Bomber

In the early 1960s President Kennedy's administration dropped plans to replace the old B52 bombers which carried American nuclear bombs in round-the-clock readiness all over the globe. The replacement was to have been the B70, a new high altitude penetrating Valkyrie bomber. The U2 incident (see page 42) had shown that high altitude planes were not invulnerable, and after 1.5 billion dollars had been spent on it the B70 was abandoned in 1966. One crashed and one is now in a museum, possibly one of the world's most expensive military curios.

Recently, the B1 strategic bomber was in a similar position. This sleek, penetrating plane could have become a crucial part of America's triad of submarine-launched missiles, land-based missiles, and manned bombers. It could also have become a costly white elephant. A contract with Rockwell International had been signed worth 2 billion dollars. The project would have provided jobs for 70 000 people working for subcontractors in nearly every state. The first three B1 bombers were authorized by President Ford in 1976, and ultimately a 244-strong force was envisaged by 1985. These would have replaced the 25-year-old B52s at a price of 94 million dollars each, a total of 23 000 million dollars — excluding the cost of weapons and a tanker fleet to refuel the bombers in flight. Such a weapon naturally becomes an economic and political controversy as well as a purely military one.

The B1 was a masterly construction of modern electronics and aerodynamics. Two-thirds of the size of a B52, with a four-man crew, it could fly 6000 miles before refuelling, could fly at twice the speed of sound, and could approach important targets like command centres and 'hardened' missile silos under enemy radar at 60 metres (200 feet), launching 24 short range, air-to-ground missiles, twice the payload of a B52 bomber, at a range of 100 miles. Opposition to this deadly but expensive weapon was extensive, causing great controversy and delay. ('Hardened' silos are specially strengthened steel and concrete underground launch pads. At present, US Minuteman missiles have a 1 in 5 chance of destroying such silos.) Technical problems, inflation and Congressional scrutiny all in turn rendered production uncertain. Many feel that the old B52s could have flown on into the 1990s, carrying a quarter of America's nuclear weapons and half its megatonnage. Even equipping a fleet of 'stand-off' planes with cruise missiles has been claimed as a cheaper solution. Others feel that, quite apart from the expense of the 4 billion dollars spent in development of the B1, it and all manned bombers would be dodos in the age of precision-guided missiles.

The super-bomber. President Reagan has approved plans to supply the B1 bomber to the USAF, despite the ban by President Carter.

The B1 represents an example of how a weapons program starts off as an exploratory concept and then acquires a seemingly irreversible momentum powered by the parochial interests of a military service, industrial and labour-union pressures, charismatic slogans and public fascination with new technology. . . .

The Air Force used to boast that its B52 bombers could drop a bomb in a pork barrel. Now it can be fairly said that the Air Force and its contractors are trying to fly a bomber out of a pork barrel. It is a revealing illustration of how the military-industrial-congressional complex goes about selling major weapons program. (John W. Finney, in *New York Times,* 25 July 1976)

Despite the willingness of Congress to go ahead, and despite the influence of the military-industrial complex, the B1 project was cancelled. On 1 July 1977, President Carter decided instead to develop the Cruise missile, concerned at the cost and possible obsolescence of the B1.

The Cruise missile

Cruise missiles, although developed from German V1 and V2 rockets of the Second World War, are air-breathing, jet-propelled, pilotless planes armed with nuclear warheads. Small and easily concealed, they are able to fly 2000 miles, and can strike their targets within 9 metres (30 feet).

The 53-centimetre (21-inch), 4.27-metre (14-foot) long cylindrical missile contains a mini-computer to read ground contours and hug land features, hedge-hopping on zigzag evasion courses at well below radar level. At 500 mph it is subsonic and therefore vulnerable to enemy planes or missiles, but its relative cheapness, at around a quarter of a million pounds sterling each, means that a salvo of dozens or even hundreds could be fired, many of which would be bound to penetrate enemy air and ground defences. Computer miniaturization, depth explosions and high energy fuel chemistry have all increased the missile's role in de-stabilizing the arms race, particularly in the European theatre.

The Russians possess a crude version of the Cruise missile in their 'Shaddock' submarine-launched missiles, which, with a range of 350 miles, can threaten US coastal targets, many of them cities. Yet they fear the immense capabilities of Cruise missiles and want them banned. Due to espionage, Russian technology is catching

The Cruise missile. An air launch from a B52 bomber, which, when converted, can carry dozens of the sleek and deadly accurate missiles.

up with Cruise missiles. The Pentagon is unwilling to concede its own advantage. In the 1977 budget, General Dynamics was given 234 million dollars to develop a sea-launched Cruise missile at San Diego, a figure double the 1976 allocation. Boeing, in Seattle, have been allocated 165 million dollars for an air-launched version, and for the first time 4 million dollars is allocated for a land-based Cruise missile. Concerned at the way Cruise could escalate tension and open NATO countries to more risk, the Peace Movement, CND and the Greenham Common women have all organized widely supported protests.

The Trident submarine

Nuclear weaponry is rapidly moving out to sea. The Russians have already deployed 13 Delta class submarines on station. They have a range of 4000 miles with their 16 missiles each. The United States is matching this threat by replacing her Polaris and Poseidon submarines with the Trident, which will greatly increase her sea-launched nuclear striking capacity. The first of these, the *Ohio*, is being built by General Dynamics at Groton, Connecticut. The *Ohio* is designed for a crew of 153, is 170 metres (560 feet) long, weights over 18 300 tonnes and has on board a gym, library and study area and two lounges. More important to its purpose are the 24 C4 missiles it carries, which tests show can reach the Ascension Island target area from Cape Kennedy in Florida, well over 4000 miles away. This almost doubles the range of her existing Poseidon submarine missiles.

Trident submarines are to go on station as soon as they leave ports like Bremerton, Washington, and will be able to hide in vast areas of ocean, increasing their ability to survive, and posing a considerable threat as well as a difficult hunt for enemy forces. Highly accurate, the Trident missiles will be able to destroy hardened targets (see page 15), and will be fitted with manoeuvring re-entry vehicle warheads (MARVs) which can avoid enemy missiles with evading corkscrew actions.

Thirteen Tridents are planned, but huge costs and massive research under way into anti-submarine warfare might result in cutbacks. Some people feel that sophisticated detection and search equipment and increasingly accurate missiles might counter the Trident's present technological advantages. An attempt is under way to develop a cheaper, smaller launch platform which would be less expensive to lose — it is called the 'Narwhal'.

The M-X missile

The land-based leg of the American Triad of nuclear delivery systems consists of 550 of the huge Minuteman 3 intercontinental ballistic missiles, of which another 60 were ordered in 1976. These are due to be replaced during the 1980s by a large and expensive mobile missile which fits in the Minuteman 3 silos. In addition, these mobile missiles are to be fitted with multiple warheads of great accuracy, with MARV adaptation, and are to be shuttled from silo to silo along miles of track in covered trenches. This grotesque nuclear 'shell game', a kind of 'find the missile', is geared to complicating detection and rendering attempts to destroy it unlikely to succeed. The missile could be at any one of a number of launching points. The M-X missile will be popped up from its silo by compressed gas, its rocket igniting outside the silo, thus allowing rapid reloading. It will carry twice the weight of the Minutemen and will be twice as accurate, but it has the capability of delivering many times the nuclear payload.

The United States has a 'public interface' problem that precludes running nuclear missiles round the country in railroad cars or trucks in peacetime. Potential deployment sites are confined to limited areas of government-owned land in military reservations. These are almost all located in the Western deserts, where cloud cover is non-existent most of the time. The Soviets, in contrast, can disperse by rail or truck over the vast areas of Siberia, under some of the heaviest prevailing cloud in the world. (William Schneider, Jr, and Francis P. Hoebner (eds.), *Arms, Men and Military Budgets*, New York, Crane, Russak, 1976)

The potential of the M-X is seen by some as turning the Triad into a Quadrad — with the result that the Soviet Union or any other enemy will find it even harder to knock away all four legs of America's nuclear force.

The SS-20

The Soviet Union also possesses a new ICBM on

a tracked launcher, and some of the missiles have already been deployed. Very accurate and far more powerful than older missiles, the SS-20 could strike Western Europe from the Soviet Union. It consists of two of the three stages which make up the SS-16 ICBM, which is classified and limited under the SALT agreements. It would be very simple to keep the third stage concealed near the SS-20, and bolt it on in minutes, ready for use, thus changing it to an SS-16, classified and limited under the SALT agreements. This weapon, like the Cruise missile, brings up the question of the borderline between strategic and tactical arms, as well as the problem of verification. Already over 300 have been deployed in Europe and against China. In November 1982 Mr Andropov threatened to step up this deployment because of the siting of Cruise and Pershing missiles in NATO countries.

The Backfire Bomber

Another example on the Soviet side is the new Tupolev 26 supersonic bomber. Over 180 of these swing-wing, Mach 2 bombers are deployed with the Soviet Air Force and Navy. A total of 400 is planned. Because SALT 2 was not ratified, the Soviet Union has increased production from 30 to 42 per year. The Soviet Union claims that it is a medium range bomber required to replace the 800 TU-16 Badgers and 200 TU-22 Blinder bombers stationed mainly along the Chinese border. Opinion in the West is that with refuelling in mid-flight the Backfire could become a long range strategic bomber capable of reaching the United States, and landing in a friendly client state such as Cuba. The air defences of the United States are not as impressive as those of the Soviet Union and a plane such as the Backfire could easily penetrate them. However, there is no evidence that an airborne tanker fleet is being built, and if the Russians intended a plane for strategic use they would have designed it as such. Like Dr Kissinger with the Cruise missile, Mr Brezhnev has personally guaranteed that the Backfire would not be sited or refuelled as a strategic arm, but in turn has demanded such a low short-range for Cruise (375 miles) that the United States has refused an agreement.

Missile parade, Moscow.

W O RULES T E WAVES?

For centuries control of the seas has been an important aspect of a nation's power. The seas are vital to trade, communications, and war. Naval supremacy was crucial in the formation and durability of the British Empire. Most world statesmen have read Admiral Mahan's seminal works on sea power. Two of America's national boundaries, and a part of a third, are coastal; 99 per cent of her imported goods come by sea. After her triumphs in the Pacific War of 1941-5 the United States was able to dominate every ocean. It was partly naval inferiority which forced the Soviet Union to back down during the Cuban missile crisis of 1962. There was no way in which her ships could have run the American blockade, and she was not in a position to concentrate any real naval strength in the area. American control of the seas was complete.

This very defeat goaded the Soviet Union into a huge programme of naval expansion. The Soviet leaders were determined never again to find themselves in such a position. At a time when the fleets of the United States were shrinking, with many Second World War ships being laid up and few new keels being laid down, the Soviet Union embarked upon a headlong course for global naval power. Under the dynamic direction of Admiral Sergei Gorshkov, by the mid-1970s they had attained what the editor of *Jane's Fighting Ships* referred to as 'a superpower navy'.

In 1962, the year of Cuba, the revolutionary 'Kashin' class of missile-carrying destroyers amazed the West. Towards the end of the decade the *Moskva* and the *Leningrad*, half anti-aircraft cruisers and half anti-submarine helicopter carriers, were added to the fast growing Mediterranean Squadron of the Black Sea fleet. In 1976 the first of the Soviet Union's aircraft carriers, the 40 000 ton *Kiev*, slipped through the Dardanelles to join them.

The *Kiev* greatly increased Soviet capabilities in this troubled area. She was the first of six projected carriers of her class. Carrying 35 YAK-36 short take-off and short landing fighter planes and 35 anti-submarine KA-25 helicopters, the *Kiev* also possesses SAM-3 missiles with a 20-mile range and 28 57mm anti-aircraft guns. She is capable of engaging aircraft from the two American carriers in the Eastern Mediterranean, launching a pre-emptive strike against, say, the giant US carrier *Nimitz*, as well as projecting forces ashore to intervene or protect their client states without having to wait for paratroops or air support from bases in Syria or the Soviet Union. The Soviet naval presence in the Eastern Mediterranean dwarfs that of the United States. In 1973 this situation resulted in President Nixon's decision both to put US forces on a nuclear alert and to restrain Israel's final offensive against the surrounded 3rd Egyptian Army.

In the past our ships and naval aircraft have operated primarily near our coasts . . . concerned mainly with operations and tactical coordination with ground troops.

The *Kiev*, the Soviet Union's first aircraft carrier, pictured in July, 1976.

Now we must be prepared through broad offensive operations to deliver crushing strikes against sea and ground targets of the imperialists on any point of the world's oceans and adjacent territories. (Admiral Gorshkov, quoted in Urban (ed.), *Détente*)

This challenge is a new one for the United States. Their vessels are finding Russian ships and submarines as close as limpets in the Caribbean, the Indian Ocean, and even in Norwegian Fjords. Russian naval bases have been built on Cuba, in Somaliland, in Angola as well as expansions of home ports like Severomorsk and Vladivostok. The Soviet Union now has offensive and defensive forces in all five of the world's oceans.

With the realisation of a wide-ranging capability for sea denial, [the Soviets] had progressed from the basic concept of defence of Mother Russia to the more grandiose capability of posing a global offensive threat to free world use of the high seas. In less than 30 years the Soviet Navy had developed from an insignificant coastal defence force to one that aspired to: 1. strategic deterrence; 2. naval presence; and 3. sea denial. Today, in the development of the 'Kiev'-class aircraft carrier, we may be seeing an effort to broaden fleet capabilities to add a fourth function, the projection of power ashore. (Admiral Stanfield Turner, Commander-in-Chief, NATO Forces, Southern Europe, 'The Naval Balance: Not Just a Numbers Game', *Foreign Affairs*, January 1977)

This fourth function is usually considered a last resort by the superpowers. They usually content themselves with parading their naval presence and uttering menacing noises to communicate with each other and each other's client states. In 1970 during the Jordan crisis, in 1971 during the Indo-Pakistan War, in 1973 during the Yom Kippur War between Israel and Egypt and Syria, and again in 1983 off Lebanon, the United States positioned its carriers in such a way as to draw attention to them and to threaten the shore. In 1971 the *Enterprise* was sent into the Bay of Bengal to signal a political message to India to stop short of an invasion of West Pakistan. At such times the other superpower manoeuvres her forces to offset such initiatives or to signal her compliance with particular demands. Whether the show of 'gun-boat diplomacy' was necessary to check India, or whether either of the Mediterranean fleets would have actually moved in support of client states in the Middle East was less important

than the effect upon the lesser powers. The aircraft carrier is still an effective symbol of armed power and possible intervention.

The United States and its allies deploy naval forces in peacetime which are and are seen to be at least equal in striking power and superior in sea-control capability to the normal forces deployed by the Soviet Union and its allies . . . . (Donald H. Rumsfeld, US Secretary for Defence, in *New York Times*, 30 January 1976)

Even so, there is considerable concern as to how the Soviet Union intends to use her new-found naval strength. There are plans in Congress to increase the United States Navy from 479 ships to 600. Great expense is undertaken with new sophisticated equipment. Although the United States greatly outnumbers the Soviet Union in naval fighter planes and combat marine forces, there are fears that here too the Soviet Union will catch up. The United States is determined that imbalance in the Eastern Mediterranean will not be repeated elsewhere.

Relative naval strengths 1983

Type of Warship	USA	USSR	China
Carriers	15	4	0
Nuclear Submarines	129	99	2
Diesel Submarines	6	160	106
Battleships	4	2	0
Cruisers	32	37	0
Destroyers	88	73	14
Frigates	82	180	20

(*Statesman's Yearbook*, Macmillan, 1983)

Superpower Muscle

Conventional Forces	NATO	Warsaw Pact
Manpower	2.6 m	4.0 m
Divisions	84	173
Tanks	13,000	42,500
Artillery	10,750	31,500
Anti-tank weapons	8,100	24,300
Submarines	190	260
Surface ships	860	1,290
Aircraft	3,000	7,200
Helicopters	1,800	1,000
Armoured personnel carriers	30,000	78,800

(NATO: *NATO and the Warsaw Pact — Force Comparisons*, May 1982)

Strategic Balance, 1983

	USA	USSR
Strategic Nuclear Warheads	9,268	7,300
Yield	3,752	6,100
Land-based ICBMs	1,052	1,398
Sea-based SLBMs	520	969
Strategic bombers	376	150
Strategic missile subs	32 (16 at sea)	62 (10 at sea)
Ratios		
Nuclear warheads	1.2 :	1
Arriving warheads	2	7
Missile megatonnage	1	2.65
Missile megatonnage with bombers	1	1.6
Hard target potential	1	1.26

World's Stock of Nuclear Warheads

Total : 40,000	Strategic	Tactical
USA	7,500 – 9,268	20,000
USSR	6,500 – 7,300	10,000
UK	192	200
France	80	300
China	4	100

(C. Chant & I. Hogg, *The Nuclear War File*, Ebury Press, 1983)

US Sixth Fleet in the Mediterranean. A jet bomber lands on the deck of the aircraft carrier *Forrestal* during the 1957 Jordon Crisis. The US Sixth Fleet has maintained a presence in the Eastern Mediterranean for two decades.

The growing worldwide power of the USSR.

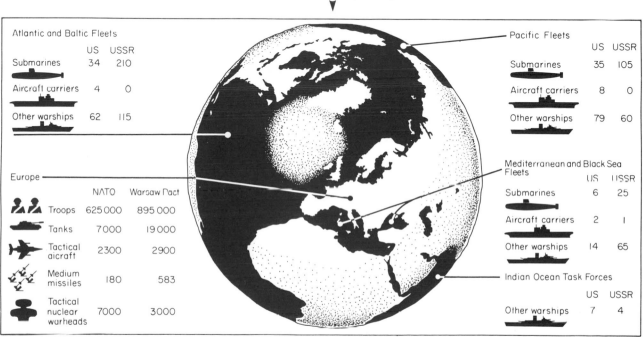

Atlantic and Baltic Fleets

	US	USSR
Submarines	34	210
Aircraft carriers	4	0
Other warships	62	115

Europe

	NATO	Warsaw Pact
Troops	625 000	895 000
Tanks	7000	19 000
Tactical aicraft	2300	2900
Medium missiles	180	583
Tactical nuclear warheads	7000	3000

Pacific Fleets

	US	USSR
Submarines	35	105
Aircraft carriers	8	0
Other warships	79	60

Mediterranean and Black Sea Fleets

	US	USSR
Submarines	6	25
Aircraft carriers	2	1
Other warships	14	65

Indian Ocean Task Forces

	US	USSR
Other warships	7	4

THE TRUMAN DOCTRINE

The United States assumed the role of champion of the West against Russian expansion as early as March 1946, with a toughened attitude to Stalin's demands in Iran. According to his assistant, George M. Elsey, this was when President Truman first 'blew the whistle on the Communists'. Truman stiffened his stand by declaring that American troops would stay in Europe as long as they were required. He endorsed Churchill's 'Iron Curtain' speech, refused to compromise on the Baruch Plan for the international control of atomic weapons, and warned against further Russian expansion in Eastern Europe. Although president by accident, he was determined to convince the Soviet Union that he was no pushover.

The policy which set the tone of almost two decades of confrontation between the United States and the Soviet Union, for long the only two superpowers, became known as the Truman Doctrine. It resulted from a warning given by Britain in February 1947 that she was no longer able to support Greece and Turkey either financially or militarily in their struggle against communism. On 12 March 1947, Truman delivered a speech to a joint session of Congress which, he later noted in his *Memoirs*, had to be blunt: 'This was America's answer to the surge of expansion of Communist tyranny. It had to be clear and free of hesitation or double talk.'

At the present time in world history nearly every nation must choose between alternative ways of life. The choice is often not a free one. One way of life is based upon the will of the majority, and is distinguished by free institutions, representative government, free elections, guarantees of individual liberty, freedom of speech and religion and freedom from political oppression.

The second way of life is based upon the will of the minority forcibly imposed upon the majority. It relies upon terror and oppression, a controlled press and radio, fixed elections and the suppression of personal freedoms.

I believe that it must be the policy of the United States to support free peoples who are resisting attempted subjugation by armed minorities or outside pressures. I believe that we must assist free peoples to work out their own destinies in their own way. I believe that our help should be primarily through economic and financial aid which is essential to economic stability and orderly political processes. . . . Should we fail to aid Greece or Turkey in this fateful hour, the effect will be far reaching to the West as well as to the East.

We must take immediate and resolute action.

The United States contributed 341, 000, 000, 000 dollars towards winning World War 2. This is an investment in world freedom and world peace . . . . It is only common sense that we should safeguard this investment and make sure that it was not in vain. . . .

The seeds of totalitarian regimes are nurtured by misery and want. They spread and grow in the evil soil of poverty and strife. They reach for their full growth when the hope of a people for a better life has died. We must help keep that hope alive. (Department of State 'Bulletin', xvi:409A, supplement, 4 May 1947, Washington, DC)

President Harry Truman. Under Truman's positive leadership the United States assumed the role of World Policeman after 1947, so checking the advance of Communism and helping to re-build the democracies.

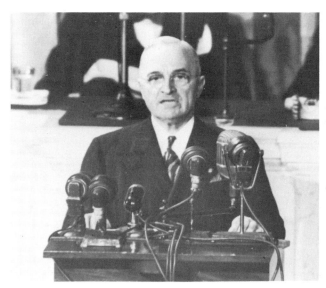

Truman's speech was a bold and dramatic declaration that the United States had turned her back on isolation and was willing to stand firm against the further growth in Soviet power. The United States took up the responsibilities of world leadership which before the war had been shouldered by the old powers of Britain and France. Truman had fused America's economic, military and political roles. His speech, worded in emotional and loaded language, was geared to making his policy seem a struggle against the forces of darkness, a world battle for freedom.

He asked for 250 million dollars of aid for Greece, and 150 million dollars of aid for Turkey, but the real aim of his request was for Americans to break with the whole tradition of their foreign policy. Americans have usually responded to a crusade, but this was a big step for them to consider taking. That it was necessary Truman was in no doubt. Dean Acheson had chillingly pointed out to him the dangers consequent upon Russian success — one rotten apple, he declared, would turn Europe to communism. Russia would use success in Greece and Turkey to control the Dardanelles and the whole of the eastern Mediterranean. Senator Vandenberg, the powerful Republican Chairman of the Senate Foreign Affairs Committee, on isolationist turned interventionist, wrote to a Congressional colleague:

The problem of Greece cannot be isolated by itself. On the contrary, it is probably symbolic of the worldwide ideological clash between Eastern communism and Western democracy; and it may easily be the thing which requires us to make some very fateful and very-reaching decisions. (Quoted in Arthur H. Vandenberg, Jr, *The Private Papers of Senator Vandenberg*, Houghton Mifflin, 1952)

Vandenberg told Truman that the only way to get the aid he wanted was to 'scare the hell out of Congress'. This Truman did, and on 17 May 1947 the aid to Greece and Turkey was granted.

Not all Americans felt that the role of global policeman was a burden that the United States should shoulder. Many felt that Truman had overreacted, and feared the complications, expense, and dangers they saw ahead in the policy he had set out. Many pointed out that Greece and Turkey were far from 'democratic' regimes themselves. Even George Kennan, head of the Policy Planning Staff, who as 'Mr X' a year before had fathered the idea of 'containing' communist power, was worried at Truman's open-ended and sweeping declarations. Walter Lippmann, the influential journalist, was shocked at the way Truman had by-passed the newly created United Nations, and wrote a book attacking the whole idea of containment and the Truman Doctrine:

The policy can be implemented only by recruiting, subsidising and supporting a heterogeneous array of satellites, clients, dependents and puppets. The instrument of a policy of containment is therefore a coalition of disorganised, disunited, feeble and disorderly nations, tribes and factions around the perimeter of the Soviet Union.

It would require, however much the real name for it was disavowed, continual and complicated intervention by the United States in the affairs of all the members of the coalition which we were proposing to organise, to protect, to lead and to use. (Walter Lippmann, *The Cold War: a Study in US Foreign Policy*, Harper and Row, 1947)

People like Senator Vandenberg saw little alternative to a positive stand, as he indicated to the Senate Committee on Foreign Relations:

I spent the evening last night with a very wise old man whom I shall not identify, but at whose feet I have often sat when I was in doubt. And he said one thing which I shall never forget. We were discussing what would happen if the United States did not follow through in the present instance, and he said:

'Well, that is a very simple question to answer. Put yourself in Athens or in Ankara. If you were a responsible Greek in Athens and you got word that the United States had said "No", what would you do? Would you not immediately say, "There is no other course left for us except to make the best terms we can with Moscow."? (US Congress, Senate Committee on Foreign Relations, 'Hearings Held in Executive Session on S.938: a Bill to Provide Assistance to Greece and Turkey', 80th Congress, 1st Session, 1947, Washington DC, 1973)

The resolution was passed by Congress and the Truman Doctrine set America's course. Greece and Turkey held off communist subversion, although not mainly due to American aid. However, both countries were now firmly in the ranks of the West, and the role of the United States in standing against further communist expansion had been clearly established.

THE MARSHALL PLAN

After the Second World War it was clear that the old powers were drained and exhausted, disillusioned and enfeebled by six years of total war. Immense demands had been made of their populations and resources. Their economies had been squeezed and drained and distorted for every effort possible. Many countries had been occupied and ravaged. Most of these older powers saw that the time of their primacy was at an end; nearly all were relieved to step down, although some took a long time doing so. Among the Western democracies the United States alone emerged from the war stronger and more prosperous. As the only creditor nation, the restorer of European peace and stability for the second time in a generation, all nations looked to her as a life-line and a protector. All, that is, except those under the control of the Soviet Union and the Red Army, whose advance into Eastern Europe was a continuing menace.

At Harvard University on 5th June 1947, George C. Marshall, the US Secretary of State, described the hardship and dislocation he had found on a recent visit to Europe and in a famous speech of American commitment suggested a policy of American financial aid:

The truth of the matter is that Europe's requirements for the next 3 or 4 years of foreign food and other essential products — principally from America — are so much greater than her present ability to pay that she must have substantial additional help, or face economic, social and political deterioration of a very grave character. . . . It would be neither fitting nor efficacious for this Government to undertake to draw up unilaterally a program designed to place Europe on its feet economically. This is the business of Europeans. The role of this country should consist of friendly aid in the drafting of a European program and of later support of such a program so far as it may be practical for us to do so. The program should be a joint one, agreed to by a number, if not all European nations . . . . Our policy is directed not against any country or doctrine, but against hunger, poverty, desperation and chaos. (Quoted in Harry S. Truman, *Years of Trial and Hope, 1946-53*, Doubleday, 1955)

Here was what seemed to be an offer free from any strings, and Ernest Bevin, the British Foreign Secretary, and Georges Bidault, the French Foreign Secretary, both accepted eagerly before the United States had time to re-think its position. Alongside the role she was assuming as guardian of troubled democracies in Western Europe, she was now to become economic benefactor.

'All our colours to the mast'. This poster by the Dutch artist Reijn Dirksen won a competition to publicize Marshall Aid organized by the Economic Cooperation Administration.

Marshall had emphasized that his programme of aid was open to all European countries. The Soviet newspaper, *Pravda*, was swift to challenge this claim, and accused the United States of yet another form of Truman Doctrine in disguise, declaring that the United States did not wish any communist countries to participate. On 27 June the Soviet Foreign Secretary, Mr Molotov, met the British and French Foreign Secretaries in Paris to discuss Marshall's proposals. There was no agreement, the Soviets were positive that the proposals were so framed as to preclude communist involvement. Stalin at this time was anxious not to allow his country's economic weakness and poor standards of agriculture and industry to come under American scrutiny. Molotov accused the United States of hopes of European domination through the Marshall Plan and claimed that fears for their exports and desire for dollar imperialism were at its root.

Although occupied by the Red Army, Czechoslovakia, Hungary, and Poland were all interested when the Marshall Plan had been announced, but under pressure from Moscow they each reviewed their position and withdrew. At the outset 14 other European countries accepted the proposals and a movement began for European Economic Co-operation. Despite considerable European initiatives the Plan became identified with the American policy of containment in Soviet eyes. Truman himself admitted that the two programmes were 'two halves of the same

American aid to Europe. This girl is checking dried egg produced at a factory in New Jersey for shipment to Britain.

American Motor. A cartoon in the Russian magazine *Crocodile* (1947).

walnut'. In this sense, while extending the influence of the United States in Europe, the Marshall Plan intensified the Cold War between the two superpowers, although Marshall strenuously denied this:

I do not have to tell you that this foreign economic program of the United States seeks no special advantage and pursues no sinister purpose. It is a program of construction, production and recovery. It menaces no one. It is designed specifically to bring to an end in the shortest possible time the dependence of these countries upon aid from the United States. We wish to see them self-supporting . . . . Whether we like it or not, we find ourselves, our nation, in a world position of vast responsibility. We can act for our own good by acting for the world's good. (US Congress, Senate Committee on Foreign Relations, 'A Decade of American Foreign Policy', 81st Congress, 1950)

In September the interested European countries had requested aid of 28 billion dollars over four years. President Truman trimmed this to 17 billion dollars at the Senate hearings on 19 December 1947. This amount was further drastically reduced by isolationist groups who were wary of American aid to Europe. The communists themselves muffled further opposition when in February 1948 they seized Czechoslovakia in a *coup*. Further shocks came in March, when Jan Masaryk was murdered, and later over threats to Berlin and, through her elections, to Italy. (Jan Masaryk, the son of Tomas Masaryk, a founder of Czechoslovakia, was the Czech Foreign Minister

and the sole remaining non-communist in the cabinet. He was found dead under an open window in strange circumstances.) The need to support Europe suddenly appeared very urgent. On 20 March the Senate agreed to the Marshall Plan by 69 to 17; a few days later the House of Representatives voted in favour by 329 to 74. On 3 April 1947, Truman signed the Economic Co-operation Act which began sending aid to Europe.

Two main agencies were set up to administer the aid. In Washington, DC, Truman set up the Economic Co-operation Administration, and in Geneva the Organization for European Economic Co-operation (OEEC) was established. Between 1948 and 1952, 13,812 million dollars' worth of aid was sent to Europe by American taxpayers. Trade, power, agriculture, fishing, and transport industries all registered improvements. Levels of production increased. Alongside such benefits the earlier successes of communism, particularly in France and Italy, declined. The economies and unity of Western Europe were safeguarded, but at the cost of increased bitterness in the Cold War between the United States and the Soviet Union.

I think the world now realises that without the Marshall Plan it would have been difficult for Western Europe to remain free from the tyranny of communism. Russia was caught off guard by the Marshall Plan. Moscow soon realised that when the Marshall Plan began to function, the opportunity to communise Western Europe by exploiting her economic miseries would be lost. (Truman, *Years of Trial and Hope, 1946-1953*)

Aid received

	US dollars (millions)		US dollars (millions)
UK	1093.4	Greece	145.7
France	951.0	Others (Belgium,	
Italy	494.2	Denmark, Iceland,	
Netherlands	371.7	Eire, Luxembourg,	
West Germany	336.9	Norway, Portugal,	
Austria	212.5	Sweden, Switzer-	
		land, Turkey)	439.4

(From A. DeConde, *A History of American Foreign Policy*, Scribner, 1963)

COMECON

Comecon is the economic organ of the Soviet Union's communist bloc in Eastern Europe. As with the United States' 'dollar imperialism' there is a political aim at root — the maintenance of socialist republics as client states under control from Moscow. 'The Council of Mutual Economic Assistance' was in part a political response to the provision of Marshall Aid to Western Europe by the United States and the resultant Organization of Economic Co-operation and Development (OECD) which was established in April 1948. Comecon followed swiftly in January 1949, and was ostensibly an alliance of equal communist states for economic co-operation. Today Comecon is responsible for the living standards of 106 million Eastern Europeans.

Although the need for economic reconstruction was even more urgent in Eastern Europe than it was in Western Europe, Comecon was little more than a paper administration before Stalin's death, meeting only twice before 1953, and leaving problems of relief and recovery to self-help by the member states. There was no formal constitution of Comecon until 1960. Khrushchev was a major influence in giving it life as an international organization. Mechanisms for joint discussions and commissions on specific issues were established and, in April 1960, a Charter set out its purposes and institutions:

Considering that the economic cooperation that is being carried out between their countries is conducive to the most rational development of the national economy, to raising the standards of living of the population and to strengthening the unity and solidarity of these countries. . . being fully determined henceforth to develop all-round economic cooperation. . . in the interests of the building of socialism and communism in their countries, and in the interests of ensuring lasting peace throughout the world. . . . Have agreed . . . 1. The purpose of the Council for Mutual Economic Assistance is to promote, by uniting and coordinating the efforts of member countries of the Council, the planned development of the national economy, the acceleration of economic and technical progress in these countries, a steady increase in the productivity of labour and a constant improvement in the welfare of the peoples of the member countries of the Council. (Quoted in Michael Kaser, *Comecon,* Oxford University Press, 1967)

Founder members, apart from the Soviet Union itself, include Poland, Hungary, Czechoslovakia, Bulgaria, Roumania, and East Germany. Albania left in 1961 after siding with China. Although splitting from the Soviet fold in 1947, Yugoslavia has been an associate member since 1964, sitting on various commissions and sending observers to summit meetings. Comecon's influence now spreads outside Europe to Asia, Africa, and South America. Outer Mongolia became a member in 1962, partly to tempt that country from alliance with China. Economic relations exist with Vietnam and North Korea. Cuba became a full member in 1972 and Vietnam in 1978. Links have been forged with several of Russia's new client states in Africa, such as Angola, Mozambique, Ethiopia and the Yemen. There are attempts under way to establish relations with the EEC, following Mr Brezhnev's formal suggestion of 23 August 1973, and exploratory talks over fishing and butter sales.

Comecon's internal relations have not always developed as smoothly as the Soviet Union would have liked. As within the EEC, there is still intense nationalism and independent ambition. Real economic co-operation and interdependence is elusive. As Mr Gomulka, the Polish leader, once observed: 'everyone peels his own turnip and loses by it'. At the outset the choice for Comecon was between economic self-sufficiency and national specialization with mutual supplementation.

Cooperation in the Council has now reached a point where it is necessary to decide the trend of the specialisation in each country, that is, to decide exactly which branches, and in what complex and on what raw material basis, should be built in each of the countries so as to meet our common needs in the most economic way. The time has come to draw up a balance sheet of production and consumption of the main types of manufactured goods in our countries for a period extending at least up to 1970, and in this way prepare a general scheme for inter-state specialisation and coordination. The intention for the immediate years is to produce the more important types of manufactured goods on the basis of international specialisation and coordination. (N. Khrushchev, in *Kommunist*, no. 12, 1962)

Khrushchev's intention of real integration, cheapening investment costs and moving towards common economies, frightened several member states. Each has clear regional or national differences, and in particular the less developed members were reluctant to give up hopes of their industrialization, remaining mere primary producers, fearing an unbalanced economy and

dependence upon other members. It was clear to Khrushchev that with narrow resource bases, small markets, inadequate labour forces, and other problems, Comecon ran the risk of low standards, poor productivity, and inefficiency. However, his integration plans did not succeed; only East Germany's economy is a close model of that of the Soviet Union, establishing Five Year Plans in 1958. Another member state often upheld by the Soviet Union as a paragon of socialist virtue is Bulgaria.

Ever-growing cooperation and unity of the countries comprising the socialist camp which in perspective will merge into a single communist entity with a common economy, culture, science, and with common social relationships — such is the trend of present time. Bulgaria and the Soviet Union will act as a single body, breathing with the same lungs and nourished by the same blood stream . . . before long every Bulgarian will know and use the Russian language along with his mother tongue. (Todor Zhivkov, 1963, quoted by Karl Reyman, 'East Europe: Sovietization at Full Steam:', *AFL-CIO Free Trade Union News,* Washington, DC, vol. 31, no. 4, April 1976)

The new Hungary. The smart and prosperous-looking restaurants and underground car park of the Hotel Suna Intercontinental in Budapest contrast with the old Buda Castle and the Matthias Church across the River Danube.

Only on Sundays. On Lucemburska Street in Prague, Czechoslovakia, many cars are covered all the week to protect their finish, since most Czechs can only afford to drive them on Sundays.

However, the degree of integration envisaged in such glowing terms by the Bulgarian communist leader has not always been echoed by leaders of other member states. Persistent nationalism and the knowledge of higher standards of living beyond the Iron Curtain has rendered acceptance of Soviet domination uneasy. Czechoslovakia is nearest to Western Europe and is the most industrialized of the Comecon states. Bulgaria remains undeveloped. Hungary depends upon engineering and food products for export to the West. Roumania's tourist industry exposes the country to Western affluence and influence. Poland has a large trade with non-Comecon countries. Of the Comecon states, perhaps Roumania, under both Gheorghiu Dej and Nicolai Ceausescu, has been the most recalcitrant and independent-minded. During the development of the Sino-Soviet split, Roumania adopted increasingly independent ways, setting up hydroelectric plants and steel works with Yugoslavia and buying freely from the West. She remains the only Comecon state allowed her own relations with the EEC.

Concerned at the lack of Comecon's cohesion, the Soviet Union attempted further integration in 1969. The Czechoslovak crisis of the previous year had convinced her that a tighter control was necessary. A 'Programme of Socialist Integration' was put forward at Bucharest in July 1971 which, to allay suspicion and resentment by member states, forbade supra-national organs and interference in national affairs. The Programme outlined 200 joint projects, of which only 12 have been realized. These include nickel mining in Cuba, copper and phosphate mining in Outer Mongolia, and copper and coal mining in Poland. The largest of the joint projects are in the Soviet Union itself. A pulp and papermill is being built at Ust-Illim, near the Mongolian border; a 750-kW power grid is being erected from Comecon countries into the Ukraine; a 1,733-mile gas pipeline is under construction with 20 000 Comecon workers using Comecon materials at 2 per cent interest rates. Many Comecon members have expressed concern that 80 per cent of their energy, oil, gas, and such essentials, come from the Soviet Union and can be shut off at the turn of a screw. There is a definite fear of dependence on Soviet goodwill. The 130 per cent price increase in Russian oil bought by Comecon members, announced in January 1975, together with the implementation of annual price reviews, was a unilateral breach of Comecon agreements. Only Roumania registered a protest.

Discontent with this form of economic imperialism has resulted in increased trade with the West. Several of the Comecon states have bloomed into a modest prosperity compared to their deprivations in the post-war years.

Country	% Trade with West		% Trade with Comecon	
	1970	1974	1970	1974
Roumania	34	40	48	40
Poland	27	44	63	47
USSR	21	31	56	49

(*The Economist*, 17 January 1976)

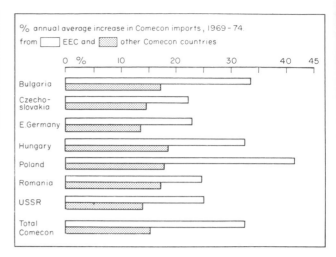

Comecon trade with the West.

General Motors, BP, Krupp, and Coca-Cola can all be found producing in Czechoslovakia. Hungary's cheap labour has resulted in 1000 co-operation agreements with Western firms, including Corning glassware of the United States and Hermes typewriters of Switzerland. Poland makes Fiat cars and has recently introduced a scheme whereby Polish emigrés may privately invest from the West in their homeland. Even Bulgaria has made computers for West Germany and has an Italian oil company operating.

However, this massive increase in trade with the West has to be paid for. Comecon states have built up a huge debt — 56 billion dollars by 1980 and possibly 68 billion by 1985. The Soviet Union alone will owe 20 billion. The consumer prosperity boom is over, there must be a period of consolidation leading to slower growth. The new Five Year Plan has halved its annual growth to 1.5 per cent. Unless the West is willing to go on lending finance and technicians for Soviet investment, the Soviet Union will have to plan for very much slower growth, possibly even retreating back to 'Socialism in One Country', or else make huge cuts in military expenditure.

Her global activities in recent years do not suggest that she is willing to make such cuts. Indeed, there is evidence of a new interest in client states far from her traditional European sphere of interest as her involvement in countries like Cuba suggests:

It is in the restructuring of the national economy that we can see most clearly the influence of the Soviet Union in Cuban affairs, amounting, in some cases, to the integration of national programmes. First came the setting up of a Soviet-Cuban Commission for Economic, Scientific and Technical Cooperation, followed by Cuba's full membership of Comecon and the announcement that the Cuban Five Year Plans for 1976-80 were to be coordinated. Meanwhile, in order to ensure conformity with the Soviet model, some 6000 Russian advisers have been stationed in Cuba. (Sir Herbert Merchant, *The Times*, London, 15 January 1977)

Warsaw Pact Defence Expenditure and Military Manpower

Member	million US $	per capita	% GNP	Armed Forces	Paramilitary
Bulgaria	1,140	151	3.4	149,000	175,000
Czechoslovakia	3,520	229	4.0	194,000	158,000
East Germany	4,790	415	6.1	167,000	70,000
Hungary	1,080	115	2.3	101,000	75,000
Poland	4,670	131	3.2	320,000	72,000
Romania	1,470	61	1.3	185,000	37,000
USSR	185,000	680	14.0	3,673,000	560,000

(IISS: *The Military Balance*, 1981-82)

NATO

The North Atlantic Treaty Organization was born out of the Cold War. In the face of Russian threats to expand further in Eastern Europe after the Second World War some military and political deterrent was needed to restrain the ambitions of the Soviet Union. The crisis over the Berlin Blockade in 1948-9 convinced the United States of the need to actively lead a European alliance of the Western democracies. The European countries themselves were only too pleased to fall in beneath the protective umbrella of the world's strongest power. The Treaty was signed in Washington on 4 April 1949, and has been in operation ever since.

The original signatories were Britain, France, Belgium, the Netherlands, Italy, Portugal, Holland, Denmark, Iceland, Norway, Canada, and the United States. Greece and Turkey joined in 1952, and West Germany in 1955. All the member states pledged mutual assistance in the event of aggression against any one of them:

Article 5: The parties agree that an armed attack against one or more of them in Europe or North America shall be considered an attack against them all; and consequently they agree that, if such an armed attack occurs, each of them in exercise of the right of individual or collective self-defence recognised by Article 51 of the Charter of the United Nations, will assist the party or parties so attacked by taking forthwith, individually and in concert with the other parties, such action as it deems necessary, including the use of armed force, to restore or maintain the security of the North Atlantic area. (Excerpt from the Treaty, quoted in J.A.S. Grenville, *The Major International Treaties, 1914-1973*, Methuen, 1974)

Opinion in the United States was far from united in support for NATO and American involvement in the expenditure and responsibilities it entailed. The Senate ratified the Treaty by 84 to 13 votes, but many Congressmen spoke out against it, and against allocating the 1.5 billion dollars immediately requested by President Truman as Mutual Defence Assistance for Europe. The alliance has experienced a chequered career since 1949, with first one side then the other side of the Atlantic partnership casting doubts on its future. In recent years France and Greece have both withdrawn from military expenditure and participation in NATO, Turkey and Greece have fought one another in Cyprus, Iceland and Britain have broken off diplomatic relations over the Cod War and Italy and Portugal have flirted with communism. The United States has openly shown its exasperation with its costly allies.

What is most worrisome is not the foreign policy of nations in Western Europe, but their domestic evolution. The growth of left-wing policies threatens to undermine the security relationship and defence policies on which the alliance has been constructed. . . . The dominance of communist parties in the West is unacceptable. . . . It is not our job to manipulate domestic policies. Our capacity is finite. But it is inconceivable that the United States could maintain ground forces in Europe if there is major communist participation in Western governments. The foundation of our Atlantic security would therefore be eroded. (Dr Henry Kissinger, quoted in *The Times*, London, 8 April 1976)

However, for a quarter of a century NATO has existed as an alliance and has helped contain Soviet expansion. In December 1950, an integrated defence force and command system was set up with headquarters in Paris until the French withdrawal in 1967, and then in Brussels. The United States usually contributes up to a quarter of NATO's budget, and the Commander-in-Chief is always an American general. Since 1957 NATO has possessed a nuclear capability, but consent by the President of the United States is required for its use. NATO has entangled the United States over the years, but that entanglement has been sought and has led to great power and influence.

"I'll carry the bar . . ."

A view of NATO, *The San Fransisco Chronicle*, 2 June 1971.

The United States backs up its guarantee to come to the defence of Europe by, in effect, extending the protective umbrella of the Strategic Air Command with the atom bomb. In return, Europe provided the bases that the United States needed in order to strike effectively at the heart of Russia. (Robert E. Osgood, *NATO: the Entangling Alliance*, University of Chicago Press, 1962)

US adherence to the NATO alliance is a recognition that Europe's freedom and strength are vital to America's own safety. There can be little doubt that, if free Europe were to fall under Soviet control, the addition of its huge industrial manpower resources to those of the Soviet bloc would decidedly shift the balance of power against the United States and the rest of the free world .... The United States has an important stake in the continued freedom of Europe from Soviet domination. Western Europe is by far the largest customer of American goods. (US Department of State, *NATO: the First Ten Years, 1949-59*, Washington, DC, 1959).

Today renewed fears as to Soviet intentions have placed a new spotlight on NATO and its capabilities. While NATO's cohesion and economic stability have been in decline, as reflected in reduction of force levels, squabbles over arms adoptions and budgetary allocations, the strength of Soviet and Warsaw Pact forces have been increasing at an alarming rate. Both the quantity and quality of Soviet weapons and troops have been improved. British Defence White Paper Estimates for 1976 showed the imbalance of NATO and Warsaw Pact forces in Central Europe as an advantage to the Pact of 1.3 to 1 in troops, 1.4 to 1 in front-line combat troops, 2.7 to 1 in tanks, 2.5 to 1 in field guns, and 2.3 to 1 in tactical aircraft. In the Eastern Atlantic the Soviet fleet had an advantage of 2 to 1 in surface ships, 1.7 to 1 in submarines, and 1.5 to 1 in combat aircraft. NATO defence budgets stopped falling and during the 1980s were required to increase by 3% annually.

Several other fears haunt NATO commanders, apart from a gradual reduction in numbers and resources. Few NATO combat units occupy their actual defence positions. Reports by serving NATO officers caused a furore when they suggested that Soviet forces could reach the Rhine in 48 hours, long before NATO units could take up their front-line positions or decide to threaten the use of nuclear weapons. Too much of NATO's forces are 'tail' and not 'teeth'; too many units are geared to support roles, fighting a long war, rather than combat roles in a short conflict. Soviet strategy is traditionally geared to a short, sharp attack carried through by overwhelming preponderance of numbers and firepower. Their leaders respect a show of strength and front-line deterrents. NATO does not offer this.

Because NATO is a coalition, there is little standardization. Ideas of national sovereignty and competition for lucrative defence contracts between members has led to a variety and proliferation of weapons and techniques. The allies' planes are often unable to use each others' bases because nozzles and attachments are not standard. Whereas the Warsaw Pact is a military alliance uniformly armed and equipped by the Soviet Union, and it enjoys definite military, political, and economic advantages.

After a quarter of a century of efforts to standardise weapons, the 12 NATO armies in Europe still have 13 kinds of close-range weapons, 6 short-range missiles, 7 medium-range missiles and 5 long-range missiles. At sea, NATO navies employ 36 types of radar, 8 kinds of surface-to-air missiles and 40 varieties of heavy guns.

NATO's former Supreme Commander, Gen. Andrew Goodpaster, estimated that improvement in standardisation could save the NATO nations 12 billion dollars a year and lift effectiveness 30%. But arms orders in the billions have proven to be too lucrative a source of profit and too susceptible to national political influences for the adoption of common weapons systems. The six national armies stationed in Germany cannot resupply each other with ammunition and spare parts and often use different grades of fuel. The United States, which has talked most about collective defense has often done the least, except when American arms, such as last year's 2 billion dollars' worth of F-16 fighters, have been sold to the allies. (*New York Times*, 23 August 1976)

Indeed the insistence of nationalism has probably been one of NATO's deepest problems. In times of economic strain member countries are reluctant to commit themselves too heavily financially. Few are ready to allow the United States to dictate defence policy, deployment, and foreign relations. Members like Norway and Turkey, neighbours to the Soviet Union, with huge enemy troop establishments on their doorstep, walk a particularly dangerous tightrope. Most members see the pitfalls of overdependence upon the United States.

In 1955 the combined GNP's of European NATO countries was only 75% of U.S. GNP. Today they broadly equate.

A common language. NATO troops enjoy a card game while resting during an exercise in Norway in 1972. The soldiers' nationalities are, from left to right: UK, Canada, Luxemburg, US, Norway, Norway, Luxemburg, Luxemburg, Italy. (NATO photo)

Then Europe spent 41% of America's total defence bill; today that has risen to 68%. Yet 91% of the ground forces and 86% of the air forces actually available in Europe come from the European allies. (Royal United Services Institute: *Defence Yearbook 1983*, Brassey)

Let me state quite clearly for all to hear — including those in Europe and this country who should know better but still tend to question our commitment to the defence of Europe: the United States is committed to the security and integrity of Western Europe, not only because it is in the interests of Europe but it is in the vital interest of the United States. This has been the fundamental bedrock of U.S. national security policy since at least 1947 and arguably since 1917. (Harold Brown, US Secretary for Defence, to Senate Foreign Relations Committee, 19 September, 1979)

It is the joint European-American commitment to share the burden of our common defence, which assures the peace. Thus, we regard any military threat to Europe as a threat to the United States itself. 375,000 United States servicemen provide the living guarantee of this unshakeable United States commitment to the peace and security of Europe. (President Reagan, 21 October, 1981)

With the mounting realization of Soviet armed power in Europe, the Cold War aspects of NATO's *raison d'être* are once again to the fore. As well as the resources to deter and defend, NATO requires the will and determination to do so. Ideals, it has been said, are also a form of power.

THE WARSAW PACT

Most great powers have some kind of an alliance system through which they can exercise their political and military might. This alliance system can be used as a deterrent, as a mediator, or as a means of exerting pressure on others. The Soviet Union's alliance system is the Warsaw Pact, a political and military union of the communist states in Eastern Europe. These were all states overrun, occupied, or 'liberated' by the Red Army at the end of the Second World War. Since then they have all remained members of the communist bloc, effectively satellite states of the Soviet Union.

Although the countries of Western Europe and the North Atlantic set up NATO in 1949, the Warsaw Pact was not created until 14 May 1955, one day before the State Treaty with Austria and the ending of the Soviet Union's right to station troops in Hungary and Roumania. The Soviet Union had feared a change in the balance of power in Europe for some time, especially after the 1953 uprising in East Germany and the 1954 Geneva talks. She determined to bind her satellite states more closely to her. The occasion for initiating closer co-ordination was the outcome of the Paris Agreements of 23 October 1954, when the restoration of the sovereignty of West Germany and its membership of NATO had been agreed. A conference of communist states was called at Moscow at the end of November 1954, attended by Albania, Bulgaria, Czechoslovakia, East Germany, Hungary, Poland, Roumania, and the Soviet Union. They expressed concern at the Paris Agreements and announced their intention of taking the necessary defensive measures. On 6 May 1955, the day after the Paris Agreements had been ratified, the Soviet Union denounced the war-time alliances with Britain and the United States. One week later 'A Treaty of Friendship, Co-operation and Mutual Assistance' was signed by the communist

states of Eastern Europe in Warsaw. It was to last in the first instance for 20 years.

The Soviet Union has always led the Warsaw Pact both politically and militarily. It began by formalizing arrangements for military control by the Soviet Union dating from August 1952, when a decision had been made to risk re-equipping the satellite armies under Soviet command and direction. Bilateral treaties were then concluded with each member of the Warsaw Pact ostensibly to meet the Pact's requirements, but also to justify Soviet troop stationing. Little is known of the Pact's institutional structure. In January 1956, a Unified Military Command was set up with its headquarters in Moscow and, beginning with the first Commander-in-Chief, Marshal Konev, it has always been led by a Russian. The Defence Ministers of member states are Deputy Commanders-in-Chief. Since 1961 there have been joint military exercises. Although there has been increased activity in recent years, the highest organ, the Political Consultative Committee, only met three times prior to 1961. Outer Mongolia has been a member state since 1959. Observer status was granted to the Asian communist states of China, North Korea, and North Vietnam but all had withdrawn by 1962. Albania dropped out in 1961 during the split with China, and formally withdrew after protesting against the Warsaw Pact invasion of Czechoslovakia in 1968.

Article 3: the Contracting Parties shall consult together on all important international questions involving their common interests, with a view to strengthening international peace and security. Whenever any one of the Contracting Parties considers that a threat of armed attack on one or more of the states party to the Treaty has arisen, they shall consult together immediately with a view to providing for their joint defence and maintaining peace and security. . . .

Article 5: the Contracting Parties have agreed to establish a unified command, to which certain elements

A divided city in a divided world. A West Berlin family watch as East Berlin border guards strengthen the wall which divides their city, 1961.

of their armed forces shall be allocated by agreement between the parties, and which shall act in accordance with jointly established principles. The parties shall likewise take such other concerted action as may be necessary to reinforce their defensive strength, in order to defend the peaceful labour of their peoples, guarantee the inviolability of their frontiers and territories and afford protection against possible aggression. (Excerpts from the text of the Warsaw Pact, quoted in Grenville, *The Major International Treaties 1914-1973*)

Past meetings of the Pact have often been a prelude to some 'concerted' action, usually at the instigation of the Soviet Union. In Berlin, in 1961, a meeting was followed by the erection of the Berlin Wall in August:

The governments of the Warsaw Treaty member states address . . . the German Democratic Republic . . . with a proposal that a procedure be established on the borders of West Berlin which will securely block the way to subversive activities against the countries of the socialist camp . . . the governments of the Warsaw Treaty states realise, of course, that protective measures along the borders of West Berlin will somewhat inconvenience the population. But the entire responsibility for the existing situation rests exclusively with the western powers, and the Federal Republic of Germany in the first place. (*Pravda,* 15 August 1961)

Similarly, the Warsaw Letter to Dubček in July 1968 was followed by the full-scale invasion by the Pact's forces in August. The influence of the Soviet Union is dominant and pervasive, and the presence of the Red Army is a crucial aspect of Soviet control. In the early days of the Pact, in 1956, only Russian troops were used to invade and subdue the Hungarian revolt, the Soviet Union being uncertain of the loyalties and abilities of the Pact members at that time. The use of the terms of the Treaty had been invoked by Kadar's counter-government, which itself had been set up and declared at Red Army headquarters. (During the uprising in Hungary in 1956, Janos Kadar, the Secretary of the Hungarian Communist Party, formed a rival Government, loyal to the Soviet Union, in opposition to the rebel Government led by Imre Nagy.) By 1968 the Soviet Union felt confident enough to involve other Warsaw Pact members in the invasion.

Soviet forces in Eastern Europe

Country	Troops	Motor-ized divs.	Arm-oured divs.	Tanks	Combat Aircraft
East Germany	168 000	10	10	7000	1100
Poland	20 000	0	2	4000	300
Hungary	40 000	2	2	3900	275
Czechoslovakia	54 000	3	2	4500	100
Total	282 000	31		19 400	1775

(Schneider and Hoebner (eds), *Arms, Men and Military Budgets*)

Non-Soviet Warsaw Pact forces in Eastern Europe

Country	Troops	Motor-ized divs.	Arm-oured divs.	Tanks	Combat Aircraft
East Germany	112 000	4	2	2000	330
Czechoslovakia	155 000	5	5	3100	450
Poland	240 000	8	5	4100	785
Hungary	90 000	5	1	1500	108
Bulgaria	120 000	8	2	2200	253
Romania	141 000	8	2	2070	254
Total	858 000	55		14 970	2180

Despite this maintenance of large Soviet forces deep in the territory of member states, there have been several attempts to improve the limited freedom of the Warsaw Pact countries. The most notable failures were in Hungary in 1956 and in Czechoslovakia in 1968. Within Comecon, Roumania has managed to develop the greatest freedom of action and the most strikingly independent line, partly because internally the regime has maintained tight control and order which has prompted no Soviet fears of her secession from the communist bloc. Since 1958 there have been no Soviet troops on her soil. She has refused to allow Soviet submarine bases to be built, allows no Warsaw Pact manoeuvres inside her borders, and does not participate in large-scale exercises. In November 1964, she reduced conscription from the generally high level among Warsaw Pact members to a much lower level. In May 1965, there was a nine-day Warsaw Pact summit near her border with the West Ukraine, and for a while she suspected some military move against her, but none materialized. In May 1966, Mr Ceausescu met with another communist dissident, President Tito of Yugoslavia, to call for the dismantling of all military alliances and foreign bases and the withdrawal of all troops stationed in countries other than their own. This stance elicited a visit from Mr Brezhnev, the Soviet leader, but to little effect. After the Czechoslovakian invasion in 1968 Roumania formed a special militia and declared that Soviet troops were not to enter Roumania without her consent. The Soviet Union was worried what would happen to this area of her influence once Tito was replaced in Yugoslavia, and Mr Brezhnev made several attempts at closer ties with Roumania and Yugoslavia, being caricatured by the Western press as 'the Big Bad Wolf'.

Indeed, despite the political and military realities of Eastern Europe, where little could prevent Soviet occupation if it was necessary, international communism has repeatedly challenged Russian domination, as did Señor Carrillo of Spain:

In former years Moscow, where our dreams began to take on reality, was our Rome. We talked of the Great Socialist October Revolution as the day of our birth. Those were the times of our childhood. Today we have become adults . . . .

The existence of new problems has made our differences apparent, has made us realise the divergent opinions among us that could not be solved otherwise but through discussion, in a spirit of self-criticism, in the recognition of the diversity of views and of national forms of Socialism and Socialist policies . . . .

It is true that we, the Communists, today have no centre that gives us directives, have no international discipline imposed upon us. What unites us today are the bonds of affinity based on the theory of scientific Socialism. We will not return to the structures and concepts of internationalism that prevailed in the past . . . .

It is necessary that the diversity of our movement is accepted once and for all and that everyone renounce all intrigues designed to undermine this fact. The differences between us will not lead to any schism provided that no one elevates his own conceptions to the rank of a dogma, that one respects the character and the positions of each party and that one maintains a creative Marxist attitude toward the changes that have developed during the period in which we are living. (*New York Times*, 4 July 1976)

Despite this feeling, the Warsaw Pact has often been used as a propaganda vehicle by the Soviet Union. The political wishes and intentions of the

Soviet Union are often made known through the Pact. Instances of this occurred in 1965 and again in 1969 when the Pact called for a European Conference, in 1973 when it suggested talks on mutual balanced force reductions, and in 1974 when it proposed a European Security Council. Article 11 of the Pact's Treaty has consistently been used to show that it is ready to dissolve the alliance if a viable system of European collective security was ever established. Fairly typical was a statement issued by the Pact after a meeting at Karlovy Vary in Czechoslovakia in 1967:

The twenty year period of the validity of the Atlantic Pact expires in 1969, and this represents a clear alternative: a Europe without military blocs. This alternative must be put on the agenda with all earnestness. No effort should be spared to develop a broadscale movement of the peace-loving forces against the extension of any modification of the Atlantic Pact. This movement is favoured by the constructive attitude of the Warsaw Treaty member-nations, who have repeatedly stated, and solemnly confirmed in the Bucharest Declaration, their readiness for the simultaneous disbanding of both military alliances. (*Pravda*, 27 April 1967)

With the increased consciousness of both sides of the danger of détente failing, and against the background of an arms race escalating to terrifying levels, such a disbanding of the alliances is unlikely. The Warsaw Pact forces are still being re-equipped and supplemented each year. It is, however, an indication of continued Soviet anxiety regarding the reliability of these forces that although nuclear missile launchers are being provided, the warheads remain under Soviet control. Even so, sophisticated and modern equipment has been deployed mainly to the northern tier of Poland, Czechoslovakia, and East Germany, where most Warsaw Pact exercises take place, and whence NATO expects that any Soviet attack would be likely to come. The experience of Poland and Solidarity since 1980 is a stark reminder of the relationship of the Soviet Union to its satellite Communist parties in Warsaw Pact countries. Europe continues to resemble an armed camp under the banners of the superpowers.

Twenty-fifth Congress of the Communist Party of the Soviet Union, Moscow, 1976. A picture of unity as Young Pioneers welcome the Party Delegates, warmly applauded by Mr Brezhnev, who later in the year bristled at the independent-minded speech delivered by the Spanish Communist leader, Señor Carrillo, at the International Congress.

THE SINO-SOVIET SPLIT

Relations began well between Soviet Russia and the new Communist China in 1949. Bolsheviks helped Mao Tse-tung in the very early days of his party's struggle in the 1920s. After the establishment of the People's Republic of China, it was only natural for Mao to fly to Moscow to conclude a Treaty of Friendship, Alliance and Mutual Assistance with Stalin. Soviet Russia could not afford to miss the opportunity of controlling another potential Tito on her doorstep, particularly since China possessed such vast man-power. Although China was hardly small enough to qualify as a satellite, there was no question of an alliance with the West, and yet help would certainly be needed. In the event, the Sino-Soviet union lasted only eight years, but this was sufficient to entrench in American minds the importance of containing these giant neighbours.

Basic security worries by both sides rendered the friendship suspect and less than wholehearted. Russia has always feared Chinese numbers. China has for long resented territorial losses to the tsars. Mao only received one tenth of the loan he requested. The Manchurian Railway and the great harbours of Dairen and Port Arthur stayed in Russian hands for some years. Throughout the 1950s the Soviet aid was a mere 2 per cent of the Chinese investment programme. The Chinese were expected to repay the 2000 million dollar loan they borrowed to champion the communist cause in the Korean War. In October 1954, Khrushchev, Bulganin, and Mikoyan all visited Peking. By the time he returned to Russia Khrushchev regarded conflict with China as inevitable.

Ever since I've first met Mao, I've known . . . that Mao would never be able to reconcile himself to any other Communist Party being in any way superior to his own within the world Communist movement . . . . I remember that when I came back from China in 1954 I told my comrades: 'Conflict with China is inevitable.' I came to

Nikita Khrushchev and Mao Tse-tung, Peking, 1954. Relations between the two major communist powers soon turned sour, and differences have ranged from doctrinal disputes to border fighting.

this conclusion on the basis of various remarks Mao had made . . . . He's a nationalist, and at least when I knew him, he was bursting with an impatient desire to rule the world. His plane was to rule first China, then Asia, then . . . what? (Nikita Khrushchev, *Khrushchev Remembers*, Little Brown, 1970)

A rift was soon seen to develop between the world's leading Communist powers. At the Bandung Conference of 1955 China adopted a key role in the leadership of the non-aligned countries. Moscow deeply resented China's emergence as the leader of international communism in the Third World. In turn, Khrushchev's denunciation of Stalin at the 20th Party Congress in 1956 shocked Chinese leaders. They found the idea of peaceful coexistence with the capitalist world abhorrent, preferring violent world revolution. An ideological clash should have been avoided, but doctrinal differences became clear and national interests grew apart. Divergent economic and social policies and systems resulted. Lin Paio spoke of the 'World Village' and the 'World City', claiming that China stood for the former, which would vanquish the more developed world. Mao himself frightened the Soviet Union by showing no awareness of the dangers of nuclear war, referring to atom bombs

'The World Village'. China prides herself on her support and leadership of the non-aligned, developing countries of the Third World. Here Chinese materials and technicians give African youths practical training in a rural machine workshop.

as 'paper tigers', and speaking of a readiness to sacrifice half of mankind for socialism. Khrushchev decided not to give China nuclear capabilities after all, anxious that the United States might arm Western Germany in retaliation, and that such weapons might one day be used against the Soviet Union. Mao further realized the incompatibility of the two communist powers when Russia failed to stand with China over the off-shore islands of Quemoy and Matsu, the Indian border dispute, and the Great Leap Forward. The Great Leap Forward was the Second Five Year Plan, started by the Chinese Communists in 1958. It was an attempt to boost agricultural and industrial production by what the Russians considered hysterical use of manpower and sloganizing — the encouragement of back-yard furnaces for steel, etc. Khrushchev disagreed with this betrayal of Russian ideas of a planned economy, scoffing that inspirational campaigns and ant-like man-power was no model. In August 1960, Khrushchev withdrew 1390 technical and industrial advisers, along with their blueprints, in order to restrain Mao and to demonstrate his dependence on the Soviet Union.

Against a background of bitter recrimination and propaganda it was not long before actual fighting broke out along the 4000-odd-mile frontier which the two superpowers share from the Pamirs to Korea. In 1962 there were clashes in Sinkiang. From 1963 the Chinese began a campaign against the 'unequal treaties' by which they claimed 1 540 000 square kilometres (594 200 square miles) of their territory had been annexed by the tsars. The Soviet Union had renounced all this land in 1920 but had never acted upon her word. Many areas are now densely populated, and the Trans-Siberian Railway, a vital communications link for Russia, runs very close to the border. Vlad and Khabarovsk appear on Chinese maps as Poli and Haishenwei, but before the Soviet Union peopled the area these places did not exist. Over 5000 violations of territory were claimed by the Soviet Union during the 1960s. Bitterness and differences increased over the Sino-Indian War of 1962, the Chinese ridicule of the Russian step-down over Cuba, and the final acquisition of the atom bomb by China in 1964.

To achieve their hegemony-seeking schemes, the Chinese leaders are pursuing a thoroughly planned and coordinated policy . . . . First, a struggle against . . . the Soviet Union . . . the main stumbling block to realising their nationalistic great power plans. Second, a struggle against the unity of the socialist camp . . . forming factions . . . which would obediently carry out directives from Peking . . . . Third, a struggle against the policy of peaceful coexistence of states with different social systems and of easing international tensions . . . the mainspring of many foreign-policy actions of the Chinese splitters is hidden in the wish for a big military conflict, while they themselves stand aloof 'watching from the mountain top the battle of the tigers' and profiting by it. Fourth, the persistent attempts of the Chinese leaders to dominate the national-liberation movement. Fifth, to flirt with the imperialist powers behind the cover of talk about the 'intermediate zone' . . . while loudly accusing others of a 'compact with imperialism'. (Leonid Brezhnev, in *Kommunist*, No. 11, 1964)

The revisionist leading clique of the Soviet Union, the Tito clique of Yugoslavia, and all the other cliques of renegades and scabs of various shades are mere dust heaps in comparison with you, a lofty mountain, tower to the skies. They are slaves and accomplices of imperialism, before which they prostrate themselves, while you are dauntless proletarian revolutionaries who dare to fight imperialism and its running dogs, fight the world's tyrannical enemies. (Mao Tse-tung to Albania: *Quotations from Chairman Mao Tse-tung*, Bantam Books, 1967)

China has indeed been building up a following in the Third World, from Albania to Indonesia. China made the most of Soviet attempts to check the Vietnamese War as betrayal. She criticized the invasion of Czechoslovakia. During the late 1960s she underwent the Cultural Revolution to purge herself of revisionism, and Red Guards besieged the Soviet Embassy in Peking. A war of words continued in which China pilloried 'Soviet Russia's social imperialism' and described the Politburo as 'the new tsars'. In 1969 border skirmishes broke out once again.

Armed border incidents provoked by the Chinese side have taken place recently on the River Ussuri in the area of Damansky Island . . . . These were pre-meditated and pre-planned attacks.

On the morning of 2nd March an observation post detected a violation of the Soviet border near Damansky Island by about 30 Chinese soldiers. A group of Soviet frontier guards, led by an officer, approached the violators with the intention, as had been the case on previous occasions, of issuing a protest and demanding that they leave Soviet territory.

The Chinese soldiers let the Soviet frontier guards approach them to a distance of a few metres and then suddenly, without any warning, opened point-blank fire at them . . . . The Soviet frontier guards accepted battle and with the help of a neighbouring frontier post expelled the violators from Soviet territory. (*Pravda*, 29 March 1969)

Thirty-one Russians and an undisclosed number of Chinese were killed in this engagement. Such clashes could easily develop and escalate. Another outbreak occurred on 14 March, and in April spread to Sinkiang. For a long time it appeared that the Soviet Union was contemplating an invasion, warning China of her massive nuclear arsenal and creating a new military district for Central Asia under a general specializing in missile warfare. China sought talks with India, Thailand, and Indonesia. By 1972 over one million Soviet troops, 10 000 tanks, and 1 200 combat aircraft were estimated to be deployed by Russia on

China's borders. There was talk of surgical nuclear strikes to take out the Chinese missiles and military establishments. However, no military action was likely. Conventional invasion would be swallowed up by limitless Chinese numbers or guerrilla tactics, and the risk of nuclear war was unlikely since in 1967 China had exploded her first H-bomb and possessed at least 70 intermediate range ballistic missiles capable of hitting Soviet cities. However, China was sufficiently shaken to seek détente with the United States and end her isolation. The United States was quick to capitalize upon this rift between the other two superpowers, and the world has since shared a triangular power structure.

On the train I heard Russian passengers quizzing the car attendants about life in Peking. Other travellers who had covered the Far Eastern leg of the Trans-Siberian route talked of seeing Russian helicopter pads and troop in-

stallations from the passing train, units of a massive garrison of 40 divisions and a million troops that Russia keeps along its disputed frontier with China. Later, I would hear of sealed zinc coffins coming back through Irkutsk in April, 1974, which residents presumed were from some undisclosed border clash. But then, in 1972, after Nixon had been to Peking, but before he went to Moscow, Russians nervously pressed me to explain why America was siding with China against Russia. So keenly do Russians feel their rivalry with the Chinese that I was repeatedly asked about our diplomacy with China, especially when I visited regions close to the frontier with China.

On no other issue did private opinion seem to coincide more closely with the official line than in the deep-seated fear and mistrust of the Chinese. Intellectuals talked of the Chinese as the new barbarians: peasants brainwashed in the fields with loudspeakers, life entirely militarized, people mindless with Maoism. That is the way press articles and television shows depicted China. It struck me as ironic that these Russian intellectuals had the same image of China that the West had had of Russia under Stalin at the peak of the Cold War. Indeed, they talked of the Chinese as the new Stalinists. The 'Chinese military threat' was another bugaboo. A Russian journalist back in Moscow from Byelorussia, a continent away from China, told me that people in Minsk were worried about war with Peking. (Hedrick Smith, *The Russians*, Quadrangle, 1976)

Soviet frontier guards on the Ussuri River. Camouflaged and protected against the temperatures of 30 degrees below zero, a Soviet patrol watches for Chinese activity around Damansky Island, where fierce fighting has sometimes occurred (1969).

THE U2 INCIDENT

The superpowers are very conscious of their image and prestige in the eye of the world. Despite vast influence and incredible powers of coercion, world opinion is courted by them. Political embarrassment or compromise is distasteful to them. Nikita Khrushchev, the Soviet leader, was a past master at manipulating events so as to achieve maximum political and diplomatic currency from them, and his skill and opportunism are nowhere better exhibited than in the U2 incident of 1960.

The U2 was a high altitude reconnaissance plane designed by Lockheed in the United States. In June 1956, the CIA began sending these 'spy planes' on photographic missions over the Soviet Union at heights of up to 14 miles. There were 30 such flights between 1956 abd 1960. The quality of the photographs obtained were such that excellent views and information on Soviet military establishments and rocket sites resulted. It was clear, for instance, that the Soviet Union was not as advanced in rocketry or as fully stocked with missiles as they had been claiming

or as the United States had feared. However, on 1 May 1960, a U2 was shot down by a Russian missile while flying over Sverdlosk, 1300 miles inside the Soviet Union, *en route* from Pakistan to Norway on a photographic reconnaissance mission.

The Soviet Union did not break the news until 4 May and then merely stated that a U2 plane had been shot down while violating Soviet air space. There was no mention of either the plane or the pilot's fate. The United States felt it likely that the plane had either been destroyed outright in the air by the missile, or that the pilot had obeyed orders and had operated the aircraft's 'self-destruct' mechanism so as to protect the advanced and complex electronic systems contained in the plane. An official statement therefore simply announced that a U2 had been lost on a high altitude weather observation flight.

This was the mistake for which Khrushchev had hoped. With his characteristic dramatic flair, attracting full publicity, he revealed that both the plane and the pilot were in Soviet hands. Revelling in the fact that the pilot had baled out complete with Soviet currency and a silencer gun from his 'meteorological' flight, Khrushchev made full use of the lie the United States had attempted to embarrass and ridicule the American government.

The point in question was the violation of the Soviet state frontier by an American aircraft of the Lockheed U2 type, which was allegedly studying weather conditions in the upper layers of the atmosphere in the area of the Turkish-Soviet border. This plane, allegedly, had strayed from its course because the pilot had oxygen trouble . . . .

Comrades, I must tell you a secret. When I was making my report, I deliberately did not say that the pilot was alive and in good health and that we have got parts of the plane. We did that deliberately, because if we told everything at once, the Americans would have invented another story. . . . [They] assumed that if the plane had

The U2 spy plane.

В З Л Е Т...   ...И ПОСАДКА.

The U2, as *Pravda* (9 May 1960) saw it.

been shot down the pilot had most probably perished as well. So there would be nobody who could be asked how everything had actually happened and there would be no way of checking what kind of plane it was, and what instruments it carried . . . .

The name of the pilot is Francis Harry Powers. He is 30 years old. He is a First Lieutenant of the United States Air Force, in which he served until 1956 — that is to say, until the day on which he went over to the Central Intelligence Agency . . . . He was flying along his assigned course, accurately carrying out the orders of his chiefs, switching his equipment on and off over the pre-selected targets, to glean intelligence of the Soviet Union's military and industrial establishments and he flew on until the very moment that his piratical flight into the interior of this country was cut short . . . the plane did fly at a great altitude, and it was hit by the rocket at an altitude of 20,000 metres. And if they fly higher, we shall also hit them! . . .

The task of the plane was to cross the whole territory of the Soviet Union from the Pamirs to the Kola Peninsula to get information on our country's military and industrial establishments by means of aerial photography . . . . Not only do we have the equipment of the plane, but we also have the developed film showing a number of areas of our territory . . . . No concocted story, therefore, can save the reputation of those who bear the responsibility for this treacherous act.

They have been caught red-handed as the organisers of an incursion into the air space of the Soviet Union such a short time before the meeting of the heads of government in Paris, such a short time before the visit to the Soviet Union of the president of the United States. I believe this is a bad preparation for easing international tension. (*Soviet News*, 9 May 1960)

Khrushchev went on to warn that U2 bases would be showered with rockets and to this effect orders actually went out to Soviet missile sites. However, there was an element of political opportunism in Khrushchev's anger and indeed the success of the rocket which brought the plane down. The incident must be seen against the background of the imminent Paris summit meeting between Khrushchev, Eisenhower, de Gaulle, and Macmillan. The U2 incident was perfectly timed to allow Khrushchev to use it as an excuse to abandon this meeting. He had been under some pressure from opposition in both Russia and China to take a more hostile stance against the West. Now he could argue that for all his efforts to develop peaceful coexistence, the United States, far from 'opening the skies' as Eisenhower had suggested, had been spying and lying. Khrushchev condemned the spy plane flights, but declared himself willing to accept that Eisenhower had not been aware of them.

On 16 May, the day before the summit meeting, Khrushchev set out his demands to be met before the talks could go ahead. He expected the United States to apologize, he wanted all future flights of the U2s suspended, and he required that those responsible for them should be punished. Eisenhower had already cancelled all such flights, and many felt that with the summit so close he should have ensured that no such risks had been taken in the first place. He was not willing to accept the humiliating terms Khrushchev had set out. He accepted full personal responsibility and went on to claim that reconnaissance was a right — pointing out drily that the Soviet Union enjoyed a superiority in conventional spies! He could have continued the official lie and denied all knowledge of the incident, but he felt that that would only complicate the situation. In the event, Khrushchev spent only three hours at the summit, demanding that it should reconvene in six to eight months' time, when Eisenhower would no longer be president. Macmillan noted that Eisenhower contained his anger with commendable self-control, but that Khrushchev stormed out of the summit meeting leaving a very hostile atmosphere. The Soviet Union also left the disarmament conference in Geneva in a similar rage in June.

The U2 incident effectively ended the 'spirit of Camp David', the rapprochement begun by Khrushchev's visit to the United States. There were renewed fears for West Berlin, resulting in a worldwide alert of US forces. Khrushchev contented himself with waiting for Kennedy to assume office in January 1961, and determined to test the young newcomer's mettle. The Berlin issue was indeed the most sensitive point of confrontation for many months. Khrushchev later joked to Kennedy that he had won the 1960 election for Kennedy by refusing to release the U2 pilot, Gary Powers, so denying Nixon the opportunity of claiming a successful deal with Moscow. (At this time Nixon was running for President against Kennedy. Since he was Eisenhower's Vice-President, he could negotiate for the release of Powers, thus claiming a success in dealing with them.) Powers was eventually exchanged for Rudolf Abel, a Russian spy, in 1962. Kennedy went on to halt further U2 flights over the Soviet Union in return for closer relations between the two superpowers — which resulted among other deals in the authorization of Russian crabmeat imports! By this time it had been established that the Soviet Union had known that the United States had been aware of their false claims to strength in ICBMs. However, the next time that U2 missions hit the headlines was in 1962, when flights over Cuba exposed the very threat of Soviet missiles only 90 miles from the United States.

Mr. K and Mr K.: Kennedy and Khrushchev, the leaders of the USA and the USSR, met in Vienna in June 1961. Behind their smiles lay anxiety over the tense confrontation developing in Berlin.

THE HOT LINE

Throughout the Cold War relations between the Soviet Union and the United States were distant and hostile. Mutual distrust, inadequate information, and the lack of a dialogue confined contact between the two superpowers to a restricted language and pattern of threats, actions, and responses. With no direct relations between the adversaries there was little chance of understandings being reached unless they were agreed by deduction from a set code of conventions, signals, and statements in the diplomatic and military power game. In such an atmosphere suspicions and attitudes became frozen and prickly. Any negotiations took place from entrenched positions and with little personal contact or acquaintance. Few breakthroughs resulted.

Khrushchev's visit to the United States in the late 1950s and his doctrine of 'peaceful co-existence' was an attempt to break the circle, but the U2 incident, the Berlin confrontation, and the Cuban missile crisis showed how far away any agreement was; these events also highlighted the potentially explosive situation between the two superpowers. President Kennedy, during the Cuban missile crisis, found that communications had the effect of causing either

Back from the brink. US reconnaissance photograph showing the Soviet ship *Anosov* returning to Russia from Cuba with eight canvas-covered missiles on board.

panic or impasse due to the time lags in contact between himself and the Soviet leaders. He saw it vital to ease the tense relations and facilitate contact.

The unusual suspicions, misunderstandings and bureaucratic delays seemed destined at first to frustrate his hopes of converting the new atmosphere into any solid agreements. Only two minor accords were reached — the exchange of weather and other information from space satellites . . . and the 'hot line' teletype link between Moscow and Washington to make possible quick, private communications in times of emergency.

The 'hot line' — passing through Helsinki, Stockholm and London, but with no kibitzers — was not insignificant. Such a communications link (originally labelled the 'purple telephone') had been under discussion since Kennedy's first months in office; and its importance had been dramatised during the Cuban Missile Crisis when it had taken some four hours for the transmission of each Kennedy-Khrushchev message, including time for translation, coding, decoding and normal diplomatic presentation. . . . Khrushchev had made his final message of withdrawal public long before it had arrived in Washington as the only means of assuring its immediate delivery. A future crisis, which could be caused not only by some actual conflict but possibly by an accidental missile firing or some misleading indication of attack, might not permit either four hours or a public broadcast. Nevertheless an agreement on communication was not as important as the matters to be communicated. 'If he fires his missiles at me,' observed the President, 'it is not going to do any good for me to have a telephone at the Kremlin. . . and ask him whether it really is true.' (Theodore Sorensen, *Kennedy*, Hodder & Stoughton, 1965)

Agreement to establish a communications link between the two superpowers was reached at Geneva on 20 June 1963. Its nickname became 'Molink', and it was installed on 30 August. Apart from its testing for effectiveness and an annual exchange of New Year greetings between the leaders of the two superpowers, it was never used until the Six Days' War erupted in the Middle East in 1967.

Just before eight o'clock on the morning of June 5th, 1967, the telephone rang in my bedroom at the White House. Bob McNamara was calling with a message never heard before by an American President. 'Mr President,' he said, 'the hot line is up.' . . . I was informed that Chairman Kosygin was at the Kremlin end. He had agreed to wait until I was at hand before sending his message. I went quickly to the Situation Room . . . Kosygin's

message began to arrive in a matter of minutes.

It expressed Soviet concern over the fighting. Kosygin said that the Russians intended to work for a ceasefire and that they hoped we would exert influence on Israel. I replied, in part, that we would use all our influence to bring hostilities to an end, and that we were pleased the Soviets planned to do the same. (Lyndon Baines Johnson, *The Vantage Point: Perspectives of the Presidency, 1963-69*, Holt, Rinehart, & Winston, 1971)

Assured on common ground, the superpowers were able to exert pressure in diplomatic channels to resolve the issue. Influence among the United Nations delegates was particularly important. Despite this collusion, no results were forthcoming, and at 6.40 a.m. the next day the hot line was reactivated. Over a breakfast of scrambled eggs the President of the United States and his advisers again conferred with Moscow. Johnson

The hot line. Work on the teleprinter apparatus for the Kremlin end of the Moscow-Washington link, July 1963.

used the contact to assure the Soviet leaders that Cairo was wrong in claiming that American aircraft carriers were being used to help the Israelis, pointing out that with such excellent intelligence sources the Soviet Union must realize this. Both superpowers continued to urge each other to exercise restraint and to moderate the actions of their client states in the conflict. In such a tense period misunderstandings and precipitate actions can quickly escalate the situation. When a US Navy vessel, the *Liberty*, was sunk by torpedo in international waters on 8 June the United States could have reacted violently and against the wrong party, causing a full-scale war. It transpired later that an Israeli warship had sunk the *Liberty* by mistake.

It was precisely to avoid further confusion and tragedy that I sent a message to Chairman Kosygin on the hot line. I told him exactly what had happened and advised him that carrier aircraft were on their way to the scene to investigate. I wanted him to know, I said, that investigation was the sole purpose of these flights, and I hoped he would inform the proper parties. Kosygin replied that our message had been received and the information had been relayed immediately to the Egyptians. Ambassador Thompson reported, after his return to Moscow, that this particular exchange had made a deep impression on the Russians. Use of the hot line for this purpose, to prevent misunderstanding, was exactly what both parties had envisioned. (Johnson, *The Vantage Point*)

President Johnson meets his National Security Council. Such consultations with his top advisers and military personnel were crucial during international crises.

However, the twisting world of international crisis was starkly shown when, despite the likelihood of a ceasefire, the Soviet leaders again used the hot line, this time to complain that Israel was ignoring Security Council resolutions and was pressing hard on Syria. Kosygin spoke of 'a very crucial moment', and the possibility of 'necessary actions including military'. Particular care was taken in translating such forceful language. The message was clear. Johnson and the whole negotiating system was being tested. The test was taken up by the American President. He immediately ordered the US Sixth Fleet, cruising 100 miles or more off the Syrian coast, to change course and approach more closely. Johnson knew that Soviet vessels monitoring the fleet's movements would relay this information to Moscow, who would realize that the United States had signalled her readiness to resist Soviet military intervention in the Middle East. In addition, Johnson replied to Kosygin's message coolly and with optimism of a ceasefire that very morning, as later occurred. The tense moment had passed.

The hot line proved a powerful tool not merely, or even mainly, because communications were so rapid. The overriding importance of the hot line was that it engaged

47

immediately the heads of government and their top advisers, forcing prompt attention and decisions. There was unusual value in this, but also danger. We had to weigh carefully every word and phrase. I took special pains not only to handle this crisis deliberately, but to set a quiet, unhurried tone for all our discussions. (Johnson, *The Vantage Point*)

The immediacy and flexibility offered by the hot line proved crucial in this crisis. There is still a need, however, for the more traditional methods of meetings, negotiations, and visits known as 'summitry'. It would not be wise to rely upon any one diplomatic ploy or communications channel.

Each of the superpowers continued to pursue what was regarded as their national interest in the Middle East, but as long as one or the other did not actually intervene the larger peace was maintained. The six day war demonstrated that Johnson understood the superpower game and was capable of playing it with determination and caution. . . . Kosygin went to New York for the UN General Assembly, and Johnson was determined to meet him. . . . The two men who probably avoided a large war by laconic messages on the hot line certainly deserved to meet, but there was another reason for the Americans. They believed that Moscow's collective leadership was ill-suited to the quick decisions of crisis management. The hot line had worked earlier that month, but there was no reason to believe that it would always be successful. (Louis Heren, *No Hail, No Farewell: The Johnson Years*, Weidenfeld & Nicolson, 1970)

The two leaders did meet, at Glassboro in New Jersey. Kosygin would not meet Johnson on a government or military establishment for fear of opinion in communist and client states, and Johnson refused to go to the UN which he regarded as a propaganda circus. They discussed the Middle East, South East Asia, nuclear proliferation, and other superpower concerns; no agreements were reached, but, as Johnson said, 'sometimes in such discussions one can find elements — beginnings — hopeful fractions — of common ground, even within a general disagreement'.

President Nixon preferred the direct diplomacy of summit meetings and shuttle negotiations by his Secretary of State, Dr Kissinger. During the Jordanian crisis of September 1970, Nixon purposely avoided using the hot line to Moscow, instead sending warnings via State Department officials. On 30 September 1971, 'Molink' was converted to satellite communication. Despite the prevailing détente of recent years the Soviet Union did not use the hot line to inform the United States of the impending attack on Israel by Egypt and Syria in 1973.

Mr Robert McNamara, former U.S. Defence Secretary, fears that a nuclear exchange between the superpowers could occur by accident. This is borne out by his own experience at the outbreak of the Six Day War in 1967 when he was serving in the Johnson Administration. He received an early morning phone call from the Pentagon's duty officer who said that the Soviet premier, Mr Kosygin, was on the hot-line and wanted to speak to the President. The message caught Mr McNamara by surprise since he had been in charge of the Pentagon for six years and he had never until that moment realised that the hot-line operated through the Defence Department and not the White House. He says he had 'quite a shock' over the difficulty of getting a message to the President.

Mr Kosygin's message took note of the United States' military moves in the Mediterranean and the higher state of alert. It said that if the U.S. intervened in the Six Day War, then the Russians would intervene and if the U.S. wanted war then it could have it.

Mr McNamara used this personal experience to demonstrate how it was possible for the superpowers to misinterpret one another and how miscalculations could occur. (*The Guardian*, 15 September, 1983)

On 12 April 1983 the United States proposed new hot line safeguards against accidental war, but Moscow replied by calling the American suggestion 'a diversion'.

THE SPACE RACE

Competition between the superpowers has extended into space. Throughout the last two decades there has been a space race, a contest to gain prestige and power from technological success. Nowhere have the scientific and organizational resources of the superpowers been exhibited with such drama and impact as in space. At the brink of the unknown and at the limit of the possible, they vie with one another against man's greatest backdrop.

Strict control by the political authorities after the Second World War turned the Soviet Union into a closed society. Due to the hostile and distant relations between the Soviet Union and the United States during the early stages of the Cold War, there was no technological or scientific collaboration and very little was known,

except through spying, of the other's achievements. The tradition of inferiority and isolation regarding Soviet technology was broken by the 'bleep-bleep' signal of the first space satellite, *Sputnik*, on 4 October 1957. This 84-kilogram (184-lb) satellite had a 58-centimetre (23-inch) diameter and was in a 59-mile-high orbit of the earth for three months, circling it every 96 minutes. *Sputnik* was a major shock to ideas of American superiority and effectively shattered the myth of Soviet backwardness.

To paraphrase a future American astronaut, Even if it was a small step forward in space technology, it was a giant step forward for Soviet propaganda and a major blow to American prestige and self-confidence. It hit where it hurts most. Where was the renowned American 'know-how', that assumption of America's God-given technological superiority bred into every child in the United States and taken for granted for so long by most foreigners? (Adam Ulam, *The Rivals: America and Russia since World War 2*, Viking, 1971)

What has been the impact of the sputniks on the world situation, on relations between the socialist and capitalist countries, on foreign policy and international relations?

It is hardly necessary to prove at length that this launching has enhanced the moral and political influence and the role of the Soviet Union in present-day international relations. It has taken the ground from under the feet of malicious propaganda regarding the alleged economic and cultural backwardness of our country. It showed the world the Soviet Union as it really is. (*International Affairs*, Moscow, February 1958)

On 27 October 1957, a Gallup Poll in Washington and Chicago found that 43 per cent of those asked felt that the *Sputnik* was 'a serious blow to US prestige'. The Chinese communists were delighted at this success, and Mao spoke of the East Wind prevailing over the West Wind. The first

'Sputnik'. The first man-made Earth satellite, placed in orbit by the Soviet Union in 1957.

Chinese commune was named 'Sputnik'. However, more significant than the satellite was the rocket which launched it. 27.5 metres (90 feet) long, 2.75 metres (9 feet) in diameter and 4 tonnes in weight, the rocket suggested that the Soviet Union possessed far greater technical and military potential than the United States had been willing to grant her. One month later *Sputnik 2* underlined the Soviet achievement by sending a dog into orbit for six months in a satellite which weighed 590 kilograms (1300 lb). The Soviets had made a dramatic public display of their technical capabilities. Neither did the vital commercial, military, and political implications of the *Sputniks* go ignored.

There began a race into space. No modern power can maintain its position without activity and investment in scientific research and development. Between 1951 and 1957 the Soviet Union had doubled her spending on research and development in science. For 1957-8 the expenditure of the United States was double that of the Soviet Union. A new intensity and urgency was pervading governments. By 1966 American spending tripled while that of the Soviet Union went up five times, equalling the allocations for state housing policies. An overall national policy was established in both countries. Massive amounts were spent developing, testing, and launching missiles and satellites. In the United States, in addition to activities in space research carried out by the military, the National Aeronautics and Space Administration (NASA) was set up by President Eisenhower.

A new form of the Cold War emerged. The first American attempt to challenge the Russian successes came quickly, in December 1957, but was a disaster. The *Vanguard* missile, carrying a 14-kilogram (31-lb), 15-centimetre (6-inch) diameter satellite which Khrushchev derisively called a 'grapefruit', caught fire on launching. The US Army, Air Force, and Navy all attempted launches, the most successful being *Explorer 1*, which reached a height of 1600 miles in February 1958. Able to send satellites into orbit, the two superpowers began reaching for the moon. American *Atlas* rockets were unsuccessful, as was the Soviet *Lunik 1*, which missed and went into orbit around the sun. On 13 September

1959, *Lunik 2* hit the moon, and in October *Lunik 3* took the first photographs of the dark side of the moon. All the 'firsts' seemed to be going to Russia. The United States pressed on with complex and costly projects, and in 1960 *Tiros 1* became the first successful weather satellite transmitting 22 000 photographs back to earth.

No effort or expense was being spared by either the United States or the Soviet Union in this new competition. In 1959 NASA's budget was 150 million dollars; by 1966 it had soared to 5 500 million dollars. Despite such massive commitment, it was the Soviet Union which scored the next breakthrough, that of putting a man into orbital flight around the earth. On 12 April 1961, Yuri Gagarin was launched in *Vostok 1* from Baykonur in Kazakhstan and circled the earth for 108 minutes. This triumph put even greater pressure on the United States to compete.

I believe that this nation should commit itself to achieving the goal, before the decade is out, of landing a man on the Moon and returning him safely to the Earth. No single space project in this period will be more exciting, or more impressive to mankind, or more important for the long-range exploration of space, and none will be so difficult or so expensive to accomplish . . . . We will go into space because whatever mankind must undertake, free men must fully share. (John F. Kennedy, State of the Union Broadcast, 25 May 1961)

He was convinced that Americans did not yet fully grasp the world-wide political and psychological impact of the space race. With East and West competing to convince the new and undecided nations which way to turn, which wave was the future, the dramatic Soviet achievements, he feared, were helping to build a dangerous impression of unchallenged world leadership generally and scientific pre-eminence particularly. American scientists could report over and over that the more solid contributions of our space research were a truer measure of national strength, but neither America or the world paid much attention. . . . America's prospects for surpassing the Soviets were poor because of their initial rocket superiority. Our first best bet to beat them was the landing of a man on the Moon. . . . The President was more convinced than any of his advisers that a second-rate, second-place space effort was inconsistent with this country's security, with its role as a world power and with the New Frontier spirit of discovery. (Sorensen, *Kennedy*)

Two months after Gagarin's epic flight, John Glenn became the first American to orbit the earth, on 20 February 1962. On 16 June the Soviet Union went ahead again by sending the first woman into space. Valentina Tereshkova was launched from Baykonur in *Vostok 6* and spent 70 hours and 50 minutes circling the earth 48 times. This became the pattern of the space race during the 1960s. On 3 February 1966, *Lunik 9* made a soft landing on the moon and sent back photographs of its surface to earth. Four months later the US *Surveyor* accomplished the same feat. In October 1967 the Soviet Union's *Venus 4* became the first spacecraft to land on another planet, and in 1968 *Lunik 14* placed the first satellite in orbit around the moon. All these were spectacular achievements avidly followed by the world.

However, the landing of men on the moon and their safe return to the earth remained the most prestigious goal. NASA was steadily closing the achievement gap with some speed and efficiency. Just before Christmas 1968, *Apollo 8* carried US astronauts Borman, Lovell, and Anders on their famous circumlunar orbital flight to the moon. The Soviets realized that a moon landing was imminent. The Apollo Project to land men on the moon was a gigantic under-

Man on the Moon. Members of the Apollo 12 team filming one another during their experiments on the Moon's surface. Despite the early successes in space of the Soviet Union, the Apollo Project was a major triumph for the United States.

taking, demanding revolutionary scientific techniques and colossal organization. The Soviet Union lived in hope that the mission would fail on the same spectacular scale, with commensurate political embarrassment.

This was not to be. Kennedy's goal of a man on the moon safely returned to earth was achieved with five months to spare. On the afternoon of 16 July 1969, one million people watched at Cape Kennedy as the huge 111-metre (363-foot), 3 150-tonne (3 100-ton), five stage *Saturn 5* rocket blasted off with the *Apollo 11* mission on board. Millions more watched on TV all over the world. The mission was to be a major culmination of the Apollo Project, landing on the moon, 250 000 miles away, taking samples and completing experiments on the moon's surface, and then returning to the earth. Since 1961 over 24 000 million dollars had been spent on this project. It employed 380 000 scientists, technicians, and skilled workers. One spacesuit cost 250 000 dollars. It was the most superhuman enterprise ever attempted.

Four days later, on 20 July, with only 20 seconds worth of fuel left, the lunar module *Eagle* landed on the moon only four miles from the intended site. At 03.56 hours on 21 July, Neil Armstrong became the first man ever to set foot on the moon. Following the Outer Space Treaty of 1967, no attempt was made to claim the moon territorially. Instead 22 kilograms (48 lb) of moon rocks were collected, tests were made, and walks were practised. At 18.54 hours the two astronauts returned to their command module *Columbia*, leaving behind on the surface of the moon their country's flag, a plaque, the badges of the five astronauts from the United States and the Soviet Union who had died in space flights, and their footprints.

The United States was riding high on such a staggering prestige success. President Nixon spoke to the astronauts by telephone while they were on the moon. There was a general feeling of euphoria. Even at this moment of triumph there came a challenge from the Soviet Union. Three days before *Apollo 11* had been launched the Soviets had launched *Lunik 15*. It was feared that this launch was somehow intended to steal the show from the *Apollo 11* mission if it appeared

to be successful. It was thought that the Soviet spacecraft's task was to collect samples of moon rock and return them to the earth without the need to land men on the moon before the *Apollo 11* mission could return. This was actually achieved by *Lunik 16* one year later, but *Lunik 15* crashed a few miles away from Armstrong and Aldrin only an hour before their lift-off. The success of the United States was thus unimpaired. On 24 July 1969, *Apollo 11* safely splashed down in the Pacific only ten seconds late and only eight miles from the main recovery ship. This spectacular achievement placed the major prize in the space race firmly in American hands.

The competition continued. Five days later the US *Mariner 6* sent back to the earth the first photographs of the planet Mars, a distance of 62 million miles away. In October 1969, the Soviet Union launched three *Soyuz* manned rockets into earth orbit on three consecutive days, with successful landings in a similar sequence. The *Apollo* missions continued to carry out experiments on the moon. The Soviet *Soyuz* flights scored important technical successes in the transfer of men between spacecraft and in the docking of *Soyuz 17* with *Salyut 4* to construct a space station in February 1975. In July 1975, there was a rare example of co-operation in space, mirroring the political détente which was being fostered, when there was a space link-up of US *Apollo* and Soviet *Soyuz* craft. Two American astronauts entered the Soviet spacecraft for a meal of borsch, and handshakes and speeches for the TV cameras.

In 1976 the United States sent *Viking* to Mars and in 1977 *Voyagers I* and *II* to Jupiter and on to Saturn and Uranus, receiving photographs back throughout 1979-80. Meanwhile the Space Shuttle programme achieved success with a re-usable manned vehicle *Columbia* orbiting in April 1981 and taking operational flights with satellites and communications equipment from November 1982. The Soviet Union also sent space probes to Mars and Venus. In March 1982, *Venus 13* landed on Venus and returned photographs. By that year 1,400 earth satellites of the *Kosmos* series and 50 manned spacecraft had been launched. Several linked up with the *Salyut 6* space platform which was in orbit between September 1977 and July

1982. Shortly before, a joint Soviet-French crew flew in *Salyut 7* and in July 1983 the first woman cosmonaut in 20 years took off from earth.

Real collaboration remains limited. Space offers too great a military potential for unrestricted co-operation. Roughly half the launchings into space have been military in objective. In the United States the Department of Defence has launched twice as many rockets as NASA. Estimates for the Soviet Union are similar. There are, of course, many aspects of the space race which have proved to possess peaceful uses — teflon for non-stick frying pans is only the most mundane of those bandied about. Weather observation, topographical studies, communications, and even archaeology are other examples of applications of space and satellite research. 'Comsats', or communications satellites, are the growth point at present. The United States and India, for instance, have agreed to use NASA's satellites to broadcast educational television programmes to 5000 Indian villages, where literacy is poor. For the relatively low cost of small TV sets and dish aerials, a huge audience could be reached for programmes vital to India's well-being, on for example, agricultural topics, contraception, and literacy. There are, of course, dangers that such a mass audience could be indoctrinated by either one of the superpowers or a client state. There are fears that space could become a new battleground. By 1983 some 4,800 pieces of superpower space debris were in orbit, including 20 spy satellites. In September 1983 the United States successfully used a laser beam from space to destroy an unmanned test missile. By 1988 the USA plans 72 space shuttle flights, 25 of which are due to have military payloads. The Outer Space Treaty of 1967 banned such weapons as nuclear devices in space, but research goes on with satellites spying out silos for missiles (they have a higher temperature than the surrounding earth), listening in on telephone calls, photo-reconnaissance and anti-satellite tactics (ASATS). Pessimists point to the possibility of tampering with climate and weather, using lasers to destroy enemy satellites or rockets, manning space colonies to expropriate space resources. These and other things will be all too possible, unless some measure of agreement between the superpowers is first reached on the earth.

THE INVASION OF CZECHOSLOVAKIA

Tass is authorised to state that party and government leaders of the Czechoslovak Socialist Republic have asked the Soviet Union and other allied states to render the fraternal Czechoslovak people urgent assistance, including assistance with armed forces. . . . Soviet armed forces, together with armed forces of the above-mentioned allied countries, entered the territory of Czechoslovakia on 21 August. They will be immediately withdrawn from the Czechoslovak Socialist Republic as soon as the threat to the security of the socialist commonwealth countries is eliminated and the lawful authorities find that the further presence of these armed forces is no longer necessary there.

The sections which are being taken are not directed against any state and in no measure infringe the state interests of anybody. They serve the purpose of peace and have been prompted by concern for its consolidation. The fraternal countries firmly and resolutely counterpose their unbreakable solidarity to any threat from outside. Nobody will ever be allowed to wrest a single link from the commonwealth of socialist states. (*Pravda*, 22 August 1968)

This announcement followed Russia's response to the most dangerous threat to her domination in Eastern Europe in recent years. It was an attempt to justify the last resort of superpower policy, military invasion.

The 'Prague Spring' of 1968 was a national attempt to throw off Soviet control and liberalize Czechoslovakian communism. It began with economic discontent and a move to decentralize the factories. Economic growth had been stunted and there were many who recalled a higher standard of living. This discontent developed into a political and nationalist threat to Soviet control of the communist countries of Eastern Europe. On 5 January 1968, the Stalinist leader of the Czech Communist Party, Antonin Novotny, was replaced by Alexander Dubček. In the liberal reforms and purge of the Stalinists which followed, a number of Novotny's protégés were forced to flee or resign. Novotny resigned as President on 22 March, and the next day the new policies were explained to the other Warsaw Pact states at a meeting in Dresden. Most of the leaders present viewed what was happening in Czechoslovakia with unease. Greater freedom of speech had been allowed both the press and the public, and many of the old guard put into office by Moscow had been removed. Such ideas could spread.

Reform in Czechoslovakia was indeed being led from the top. The new President was General Svoboda, a 72-year-old war hero who had commanded the Czech Legion alongside the Red Army. Purged by Stalin in the early 1950s, he had been reduced to bookkeeping on a government estate. He supported Dubček's policies of reform and liberalization, as did Cernik, the new Prime Minister, and Smrkovsky, the Chairman of the National Assembly. The power of the Communist Party was to be reduced, along with that wielded by economic bureaucrats. The judiciary and the secret police were both to be reformed. The Czech people responded with excitement to the debate on the new nature of their state.

It was not to last. Russian leaders failed to be persuaded by Dubček that he intended no breakaway from communism. On 8 May the Warsaw Pact states met again to review the situation but this time the Czechs refused to attend. One week later Warsaw Pact forces began manoeuvres on the Polish border with Czechoslovakia. Visits were made to Prague by both Soviet Prime Minister Kosygin and Marshal Grechko, the Soviet Commander-in-Chief. The Czech leaders persistently declared their friendship and alliance with the Soviet Union and the other Pact states. They complained, however, at the prolonged presence of Soviet troops on their border. On 15 July another meeting of the Warsaw Pact drafted a letter to the Czech leaders which amounted to an ultimatum:

The development of events in your country evokes deep

The grasp of the Soviet Union. This poster was displayed all over Prague by Czech citizens shocked by the invasion of 1968. It depicts the hand of the Soviet Union as that of a beast, stamped with a swastika, and suggests that the other Warsaw Pact members who participated in the invasion are mere fingers of the beast.

countries, which have joined in the Warsaw Treaty, to safeguard the independence and peace and security in Europe, and to place an insurmountable barrier against the intrigues of the imperialist powers, against aggression and revanchism . . . .

We express the conviction that the Communist Party of Czechoslovakia, conscious of its responsibility, will take the necessary steps to block the path of reaction. In this struggle you can count on the solidarity and assistance of the fraternal socialist countries. (*Pravda*, 19 July 1968)

A week later Dubček refused a summons to Moscow by Mr Brezhnev. However, at Cierna, in Eastern Slovakia, on 29 July, sixteen Czech leaders met for three and a half days of ideological talks with the entire Soviet Politburo. This was the first time the Politburo had ever left Russia, crossing the border in thirteen car loads. Dubček declared: 'All is well. We shall not retreat a single step.' On 3 August, in the Slovak capital of Bratislava, a ten-page document was published which declared a national form of communism, but denied any split with the Soviet bloc. During the next fortnight both Tito of Yugoslavia and Ceausescu of Roumania, both dissident communist leaders, visited Prague, but whether to warn or congratulate Dubček is not clear.

During the night of 20-21 August Warsaw Pact forces crossed the borders of Czechoslovakia on the pretext of a threat from West Germany and counter-revolution. The invasion forces included units from East Germany, Poland, Hungary, and Bulgaria as well as from the Soviet Union. Preparations for the invasion had been carefully disguised by a series of military exercises and manoeuvres all over Eastern Europe. As early as June a Soviet communications centre had been established near Prague airport and intelligence had been collected with regard to access routes into Czechoslovakia. Exercises involving vast deployments of reserves, supplies, tanks, oil, and ammunition in the unusual east-west direction were undertaken. Bulgarian troops were deployed to Hungary by sea to avoid over-flying Roumania, which stoutly refused to participate. On the evening of 20 August NATO radar stations in West Germany were jammed. A 'tourist' flight from Russia landed at Prague airport and 52 KGB officials discarded civilian clothes and took

anxiety in us. It is our profound conviction that the offensive of the reactionary forces, backed by imperialism, against your party and the foundations of the social system in the Czechoslovak Socialist Republic threatens to push your country off the road of socialism and that it is consequently jeopardising the interests of the whole socialist system . . . .

We neither have had, nor do we have, the intention of interfering in such matters as are strictly the internal business of your party and your state, or of violating the principles of respect, independence and equality in the relations among communist parties and socialist countries. . . .

At the same time we cannot agree to have hostile forces push your country away from the road of socialism and create the danger of Czechoslovakia being severed from the socialist community. This is something more than your own concern. It is the common concern of our

over the control tower to help land airborne divisions of the Warsaw Pact forces. This process was in operation at other airports in Czechoslovakia. Three army groups crossed the Czech border at eighteen points and swiftly took up key positions around road, rail, and communications centres. The invasion was completed within a few hours.

Realizing the efficiency and totality of the invasion, General Svoboda appealed to his people for restraint, and there was no popular rising. There were a few skirmishes at barricades and around the Prague Radio Station, but nothing to compare with the violence in Hungary in 1956. Indeed, then the Russians had lost 7 000 men and killed 27 000 Hungarians in suppressing the revolt. In 1968 only 72 Czechs died and 702 were wounded between 20 August and 3 September. Passive hostility there certainly was. Invading tank crews, bewildered by what they had been told was another exercise, were barracked and insulted. Dubček and other Czech leaders were swiftly arrested and taken to Moscow. They were saved by the massive demonstrations of support for them in Czechoslovakia and the defiance shown to Soviet threats by Svoboda, who at one stage tore off his high Soviet decorations and

threw them on the table, threatening to commit suicide and so face the Soviets with a martyrdom. He refused to collaborate in forming a 'Workers' and Peasants' Government' for the Soviets as a puppet regime, and on 27 August the Soviets had to restore Dubček, albeit under very close surveillance and with strict orders.

There had been some underground TV and radio activity, as well as illegal press hand-outs circularized, but from the start open hostilities were useless. Youths surrounded and chanted at tanks, street signs were changed, and anti-Soviet slogans were daubed on walls. Morale was surprisingly high. China, Yugoslavia, Albania, and Roumania all registered their protests at this invasion of a socialist ally. The countries of the West also protested, but did nothing. The United States cancelled negotiations on arms limitations and stopped a visit by President Johnson to Moscow.

There was litttle we could do except watch and worry. . . . We had no treaty commitments, of course. NATO would

'Russians, go home!' In Prague all the sign posts were obliterated apart from those pointing to Moscow. The walls are daubed with anti-Soviet slogans. Tanks patrol the streets.

not support military action. The Czechs themselves had indicated they did not plan to resist with military force, and that they would not welcome any response from the West. We could only try to avoid any action that would further inflame the situation. (Johnson, *The Vantage Point*)

There was a very different reaction in the Soviet Union itself:

Beyond the substantial indifference to the invasion on the part of the masses, many people evidently took great pride in the exercise of Soviet power in the same way that nineteenth century Englishmen took pride in maintaining their imperial domain. It was one of the attributes of being a superpower. A Russian writer I know was vacationing at Sochi, in August, 1968, when Soviets began to get wind of the invasion from Western radio broadcasts. 'The people down there were really very happy with what happened,' he recalled, ' "Finally," they said, "our troops have gone into Czechoslovakia. We should have done that a long time ago. Now we must go on and do the same in Roumania." These people were glad to see that Russia had used its force. They respect that force very much. They like to see Russian power exercised.' Gennadi, the state farm accountant, said this was true among the state farm officials and farm workers he knew, as well. 'They believed the huge wild lie that the Soviet Union had to invade Czechoslovakia to help the people there,' he said. '[The intervention] was a matter of pride in their own nation. (Smith, *The Russians*)

The occupying forces began to be withdrawn on 3 September. On 13 September the National Assembly revoked its reforms and re-imposed censorship. Czech leaders agreed to co-ordinate their future policies with orders from Moscow. 70 000 Soviet troops were to remain for the indefinite future. Ironically, on 28 October 1968, the Czechoslovak peoples were to have celebrated their fiftieth Anniversary as an independent state. This event was dulled by the appearance in official Soviet communiqués of what became known as the 'Brezhnev Doctrine', or 'the doctrine of limited sovereignty':

It should be stressed that even if a socialist country seeks to take up an 'extra-bloc' position, it in fact retains its independence thanks precisely to the power of the socialist commonwealth — and primarily to its chief force, the Soviet Union — and the might of its armed forces. The weakening of any link in the world socialist system has a direct effect on all the socialist countries, which cannot be indifferent to this. Thus, the anti-socialist forces in Czechoslovakia were in essence using talk about the right to self-determination to cover up demands for so-called neutrality and the CSR's withdrawal from the socialist commonwealth. But implementation of such 'self-determination', i.e. Czechoslovakia's separation from the socialist commonwealth, would run counter to Czechoslovakia's fundamental interests and would harm the other socialist countries. Such 'self-determination' as a result of which NATO troops might approach Soviet borders and the commonwealth of European socialist countries might be dismembered in fact infringes on the vital interests of these countries' peoples, and fundamentally contradicts the right of these people to socialist self-determination. (S. Kovalev, in *Pravda*, 26 September 1968)

By April 1969, Alexander Dubček had been removed as leader of the Czech Communist Party and relegated to a minor Forestry Commission post in a rural area. On 6 May 1970, the Czechs were forced to agree to a new treaty which stated their errors, thanked the Soviet Union for their help, and further pledged Czech support against any enemy so designated by the Soviet Union. The 'Prague Spring' was at an end. The Soviet Union had demonstrated her complete control of Eastern Europe, and there are some in the West who fear the instability and crises which might develop if this were not so. It has been suggested that Eastern Europe is a necessary and legitimate sphere of Soviet domination. However, support from people such as those who signed and demonstrated for the document known as 'Charter 77', which demanded greater freedom, shows that this feeling is far from universal. The promise of the 'Prague Spring' has not been forgotten although the Polish experience with the suppression of Solidarity and the harassment of Lech Walesa since 1980 offers a dismal prospect, despite his award of the 1983 Nobel Peace Prize.

THE VIETNAM PEACE MOVEMENT IN THE US

Even superpowers have to be mindful of public opinion and the feelings of their own citizens. Controversy and opposition at home can undermine and weaken credibility abroad. The war in Vietnam had never been a popular war in the United States and the steady growth of opposition to it is a good example of how a superpower must in part be sensitive to the views and wishes of domestic opinion.

By the mid-1960s American involvement in the war in Vietnam was a major issue. As the war dragged on and escalated in scope it was increasingly questioned. Public distaste grew. With the end of the Cold War and the stirring of détente many Americans failed to see the need for domino interpretations or containment theories. Lyndon Johnson declared that he would not send 'American boys' to die in 'Asian wars'. Once committed after the 'Gulf of Tonkin incident' when US naval vessels were directly attacked in August 1964, more and more American families felt themselves intimately affected. Many 'American boys' did indeed begin to die in 'Asian wars'.

Opposition developed on many levels. The resolution which followed the Gulf of Tonkin incident was itself a controversial piece of legislation. It now appears that United States forces had been provoking such an attack for some time, and that President Johnson's resolution had been constructed and engineered for just such an eventuality, should deeper American action in the fighting become necessary. It is still not clear whether the USS *Maddox* had actually been attacked in the Gulf of Tonkin by North Vietnamese patrol boats. In any event only two Senators opposed the resolution of 7 August 1964, which allowed the President to take any measures he thought necessary to defend American interests and allies in the area. Constitutional objections to the emergency powers thus bestowed upon the President under such circumstances were a consistent and powerful rallying point for future criticism of the war and its conduct. Reports during Eisenhower's administration as to the viability of the United States fighting a successful war against communism were now ignored, and the American effort sank deeper into the military quagmire.

The economic costs of the war also soon became clear. In 1966 it was estimated that the war in Vietnam was costing 30 000 million dollars a year. Senator Hartke worked out that the cost of each Viet Cong soldier killed in one Mekong Delta action was 8 hundred thousand dollars. Johnson disclaimed such figures, stating that they were triple the actual cost. So anxious was he to conceal the cost of the war that urgently needed tax increases (which would have exposed the situation) were delayed a year, thus helping to start an inflation which would only fuel public discontent.

My own view is that there is a kind of madness in the facile assumption that we can raise the many billions of dollars necessary to rebuild our schools and cities and public transport and eliminate the pollution of air and water while also spending tens of billions to finance an 'open-ended' war in Asia. But even if the material resources can somehow be drawn from an expanding economy, I do not think that the spiritual resources will long be forthcoming from an angry and disappointed people. (Senator J. William Fulbright, *The Arrogance of Power*, Random House, 1967)

It was on a humanitarian level that public distaste for the war in Vietnam became most obvious. American casualities soared from 2 000 in 1965 to 5 000 in 1966 and 14 000 by 1968, reflecting with each leap the increased commitment of ground forces. By March 1968, there were 535 000 Americans in Vietnam. Eventually 56 226 would have lost their lives. Every bereaved American family and every wounded veteran returning home brought the war and its increasing horrors closer. The quality of the American support facilities and field medicine teams resulted in a much higher survival rate, leading to an ever-growing number of maimed and embittered casualties. When they stopped to think of them Americans found the Vietnamese casualty figures even more appalling. In so far as statistics can be verified in such a war it seems likely that at least half a million South Vietnamese died in the fighting, possibly another million were injured, and another 2 million were made refugees.

Such casualties, coupled with the moral conflict many Americans felt over devastating a distant land to save its inhabitants from an opposing ideology, also undermined the war effort. The United States began to doubt its crusade among the paddy fields and jungles of South East Asia. They found that very often those whom they felt they were protecting wished only to be left alone, and at night might even be those who attacked them. As the terrible toll of the war on the land and its people became ever more graphic, justification for it seemed to evaporate.

Hatred and suspicion of the way in which Americans were sent to fight in the war heightened the opposition. The draft was everywhere disliked. There was widespread draft evasion and burning of draft cards. Many young draftees fled abroad, hid or took positions which offered deferment. Protests and outcries were voiced against the high percentage of manual workers and blacks sent to fight in Vietnam, particularly to front-line duties. Even so, for several years the opponents of the war were a minority. Most Americans accepted the war and their role in it.

Too little attention has been given to the public acceptance of the war during most of the Johnson years. The anti-war demonstrators were vocal, but a minority. Much was heard of deserters and youngsters fleeing to Canada to avoid the draft, but the overwhelming majority quietly did what was required of them. I can remember driving down to Charlottesville, Virginia, after the 1967 March on the Pentagon. On the way I stopped at Culpeper for a cup of coffee and was attracted by the sound of martial music. About thirty young men were boarding a bus for a military induction centre. A high school band played, volunteers handed out coffee, cokes, and doughnuts, and parents and girl-friends clustered about the bus.

There were some tears, and pride. Above all there was acceptance. The young men were going away to do their duty, as their fathers had done before. I saw similar scenes a dozen or more times across the country, and there must have been thousands of them. As far as I know, they never attracted the television cameras, and local papers are rarely if ever read in New York. (Heren, *No Hail, No Farewell*)

Yet each year brought renewed commitments of more troops and hence more casualties. There seemed to be little territorial gain. The Tet Offensive underlined this.

For the first time the patience, durability and resilience of the enemy became clear to millions of Americans. . . . For the first time they fought in cities, which meant that day after day American newspapermen, and more important, television cameramen, could reflect their ability, above all their failure to collapse according to American timetables. . . . The Tet Offensive had stripped Johnson naked on the war, his credibility and that of his Administration were destroyed. (David Halberstam, *The Best and the Brightest*, Random House, 1972)

Nixon came into office pledged to 'end the war and win the peace'. The war continued. In November 1969, news of the My Lai massacre, hushed up since its occurrence on 16 March 1968, rocked America. Several hundred men, women, and children in a village code-named 'Pinkville' by the United States Army had been slaughtered during a mistaken raid on what was thought to be a Viet Cong stronghold. On 16 November a quarter of a million people marched from the Arlington Military Cemetary to the White House in protest at the continuation of the war. The march lasted for 40 hours. Rallies and protests were now being held regularly all over the country.

The October 15th (anti-war) moratorium — backed by college presidents, religious leaders, and a long list of Democratic Senators — even those who had not been in the forefront of the anti-war movement — was a dramatic portrait of America's participation in an endless and unpopular war. All across the country, the day was marked by silent vigils, prayer meetings and peaceful protest marches. In Washington tens of thousands of demonstrators — students, housewives, professional people, many of them wearing black armbands — gathered at the Washington Monument to hear anti-war speeches and then marched peacefully to the White House. In a number of cities flags were at half mast. Classes were cancelled at hundreds of colleges and universities. (Marvin and Bernard Kalb, *Kissinger*, Little Brown, 1974)

Far from ending the war Nixon and Kissinger had presided over the invasion and bombing of Cambodia, actions which precipitated a further wave of protest. On 4 May 1970, National Guardsmen shot and killed four student demonstrators on the campus at Kent State University in Ohio. On 15 May, two students were shot dead and 11 injured at the all-black Jackson State College in Mississippi when State highway patrolmen had been called in. Many colleges were forced to close. Several officials in the administration at the White House resigned.

In June 1971, further shocks to American morale were delivered by the 'Pentagon Papers' disclosures by Daniel Ellsberg, a researcher from MIT (Massachusetts Institute of Technology) who had worked for the Department of Defence in Vietnam. In the 'Pentagon Papers' he exposed the lies and secrecy surrounding the development of American involvement in Vietnam from 1954 to 1968. Most Americans were disillusioned and angered by these revelations. Morale in Vietnam was even lower. Symptoms of this could be found in the prevalence of drug-taking, desertion, and 'fragging' (the killing or injuring of their superiors with fragmentation grenades) among frontline troops. Moreover, by May 1972, continued air bombing was costing the United States 20 million dollars each day. The war had to be brought to a close.

By January 1973, Nixon and Kissinger had finalized a ceasefire date and had arranged for the phased withdrawal of United States forces. What Nixon referred to as 'Peace with honour' was to become effective from 27 January. The fighting continued, however, and the communists continued to press south. When their final offensive came in April 1973, the President admitted that there had been secret assurances to President Thieu of South Vietnam that the United States would intervene in full military strength if the ceasefire was contravened. Congress and American public opinion would not support further aid, however, and the last American personnel scrambled out of Saigon in helicopters a few hours before North Vietnamese tanks rolled in, on 30 April 1973.

The anti-war lobby in the United States was crucial in ceasing American involvement. It called upon telling constitutional, economic, military, political, and moral arguments in its struggle to end the war. Today Vietnam is generally regarded as America's single largest post-war mistake. It has been called the wrong war, in the wrong place at the wrong time. The fear is now, by both those who fought and those who criticized the war, that its legacy will cripple and demoralize future American exercise of its superpower status.

'Showing the flag'. A forlorn US Marine radioman shelters from the fighting behind the Citadel Wall at Hue.
American morale sank lower and lower during the involvement in Vietnam.

THE MAYAGUEZ INCIDENT

From time to time a superpower must be seen to exercise its strength. It must be seen to be ready to act. Diplomatic pressure, threats, and bluffs may not always suffice, and in time they may become regarded as mere trappings of power without substance or resolution. Power requires periodic demonstration, particularly if it is in doubt. Such a moment came for the United States a few weeks after defeat had been admitted in Vietnam. American military and diplomatic presence had been withdrawn, and world opinion disputed the willingness of the American people to continue to use them elsewhere in furtherance of American interests or in support of allies at risk. A new wave of isolationism, of withdrawal from the world stage, was widely forecast. The forceful action carried out by the United States

'Goliath is still Goliath'. A cartoon from the *Frankfurter Allgemeine Zeitung*, **shown in the** *Economist,* **24 May 1975.**

during the crisis known as the *'Mayaguez* incident' allayed these fears and served notice that the United States intended to continue her role as a world leader.

On 12 May 1975, communist naval vessels from Cambodia, recently fallen to the Khmer Rouge insurgents, seized the US container cargo ship *Mayaguez*. The *Mayaguez* was in the Gulf of Siam, 60 miles off the Cambodian coast, and in these waters the international limit starts at 50 miles off the coast. Conditions in the area were confused, due to the recent fighting, but a few days before a Panamanian ship had been seized and a South Korean ship had been fired upon. It is possible that the seizure of the *Mayaguez* was the action of a local commander, but it is more likely that it was a direct provocation to test American morale. *En route* from Hong Kong to Sattahip in Thailand, the *Mayaguez* was taken with her crew of 39 to the port of

Kompong Song. (It appeared that another *Pueblo*-type incident was about to begin.)

United States government officials first heard of the ship's seizure at 5.03 a.m. President Ford was informed at 7.40 a.m. and immediately ordered an aircraft carrier task force into the area. At 2 p.m. he warned Cambodia of 'the most dire consequences' which could follow such an act of piracy. At 4.30 p.m. a note was sent to the Chinese officials who had agreed to act as intermediaries, repeating this warning.

The situation remained tense and uncertain until 8.30 p.m. on 13 May, when American aircraft sank three Cambodian gunboats guarding the *Mayaguez*. The American fear was that these gunboats would be used to tow the captured vessel into shore and up a river sanctuary out of range of a clear rescue attempt. In 1968 the *Pueblo* and its crew were in North Korean hands for almost a year; such a humiliating situation had to be avoided at all costs. US marine forces were put on alert as the aircraft carrier task force approached the Gulf of Siam. The Secretary of State, Dr Henry Kissinger, spoke openly of the possibility of using B52 bombers to force the Cambodians to relinquish the captive vessel.

The next day the United States began retaliatory air strikes against Cambodian bases, such as the Khmer Rouge air support station at Ream. It has become clear that a Chinese diplomat, working through a neutral, had asked him to convey to the United States hope of the release of the *Mayaguez* and her crew a full 14 hours before final rescue operations were mounted by the United States. At 7.07 p.m. on 14 May the Cambodian authorities broadcast their agreement to release the *Mayaguez*, but a US Marine strike force had already been sent in.

At 7.09 p.m. marines from the US destroyer *Holt* landed on Koh Tang island, where the *Mayaguez* was being held captive, and after some fighting secured the ship. At 10.23 p.m. an American plane giving air cover spotted the crew of the Mayaguez in a fishing boat under a white flag. The crew had not been held captive on the ship, but elsewhere. If they had been on the ship, they would have been in great jeopardy, and loss of life might well have been greater. Forty-one US marines were killed in the rescue mission, and 50 were wounded. Three helicopters were lost. Many Cambodian aircraft were destroyed in air strikes by American planes. However, the *Mayaguez*, her crew of 39, and American military resolution and effectiveness were all intact.

There was a storm of reaction. On 17-18 May students rioted outside the American Embassy in Bangkok, protesting against the use of American bases in Thailand to recover the *Mayaguez*. Indignation was all the stronger since the United States, following requests from the Thai authorities in the wake of the fall of Cambodia and South Vietnam, had only just agreed to withdraw all its forces from Thailand on 1 May. On 19 May the United States officially apologized to Thailand for involving her in the action against her wishes. Thailand borders Cambodia and was

Crisis briefing. President Ford puts a question to Dr Kissinger during a top level meeting to discuss the *Mayaguez* incident. It was vital that the Administration stay in close contact with events thousands of miles away.

The rescue of the *Mayaguez*. **After a US Marine assault, the US destroyer** *Holt* **tows the container vessel** *Mayaguez* **to safety from Koh Tang.**

anxious not to be seen as an accomplice in the rescue.

Elsewhere in the world there were many client states of the United States who felt relieved and reassured that American power would still be exercised if required. To many, however, President Ford's decisions seemed precipitate and dangerous. To them the rescue mission seemed an immature political reaction of military over-kill to compensate for failure and defeat in South East Asia. They pointed out that more marines lost their lives than crew members were saved. In October 1976, a report by the Government Accounting Office decided that reaction had been too precipitate:

Question from Mr Valeriani: 'Mr President, the Government Accounting Office has just put out a report suggesting that you shot from the hip in the Mayaguez rescue mission and that you ignored diplomatic messages that a peaceful solution was in prospect. Why didn't you do more diplomatically at the time?'

Answer from President Ford: '. . . I can assure you that if we had not taken the strong and forceful action that we did, we would have been criticized very, very severely for sitting back and not moving.

'Captain Miller is thankful. The crew is thankful. We did the right thing. It seems to me that those who sit in Washington 18 months after the incident are not the best judges of the decision-making process that had to be made by the National Security Council and by myself at the time the incident was developing in the Pacific.

'Let me assure you that we made every possible overture to the People's Republic of China and through them to the Cambodian Government. We made diplomatic protests to the Cambodian Government through the United Nations. Every possible diplomatic means was utilized. But at the same time, I had the responsibility, and so did the National Security Council, to meet the problem at hand. And we handled it responsibly and I think Captain Miller's testimony to that effect is the best evidence.' (Transcript of President Ford's TV debate on foreign policy with Presidential candidate Jimmy Carter, *New York Times*, 7 October 1976)

Despite a certain thrill at the exercise of their power, similar to that experienced by the Russians in 1968, many Americans did feel that President Ford had indeed overstepped his powers as laid down in Section 4 of the War Powers Act. Executive military action had been taken without Congressional consent four times in almost as many weeks, the other occasions being the military evacuations from Da Nang, Saigon, and Phnom Penh. In such urgent military operations speed is essential, but there were many who feared that involvement in another scarring land war could result from unauthorized presidential actions.

The glory faded pretty fast after the four days of the Mayaguez . . . the lesson of lawlessness is the worst of all. A specific statute, passed in 1973 and still on the books flatly forbids 'combat activities by US military forces in or over or from off the shores of North Vietnam, South Vietnam, Laos or Cambodia.' President Ford did not mention that statute in ordering action; that, on its face, violated the law. Hardly anyone raised an eyebrow either — just after Vietnam and Watergate. (Anthony Lewis, in *New York Times*, 10 May 1976)

ANGOLA

Any sudden or dramatic change in the global power balance, or even in the territorial presence of the superpowers, is likely to create a critical situation. This was so when the Russian-backed MPLA forces seized control in Angola in January 1976. Shock waves were sent shuddering across the world and fears of a renewed Soviet drive for confrontation with the United States were widespread.

It was an improbable locus for a superpower collision. But the shape and location, if not the history and social reality of Angola were being firmly impressed upon the minds of millions of American television viewers. At issue, they learned from the Secretary of State, testifying before a Senate sub-committee on African affairs, was the basic principle: 'the Soviet Union must not be given any opportunity to use forces for aggressive purposes without running the risk of conflict with us.'

Angola was to be the post-Vietnam testing ground of will and power in the face of the global expansion of a bullish rival whose recently exercised military outreach was seen to be leading it towards dangerous adventures. (John A. Marcum, 'The Lessons of Angola', *Foreign Affairs*, vol. 54, no. 3, April 1976)

Angola had been a little-heard-of Portuguese colony since 1483, but for 14 years 60 000 troops had been needed to control the demands and the actions of rival liberation movements. Distaste for this colonial war helped bring on a *coup* in Portugal in April 1974. Angola received her independence on 11 November 1975, amidst heavy fighting between the three liberation movements, the MPLA, the FNLA, and UNITA.

These warring groups were eagerly wooed by the superpowers. Lying along the Atlantic coast Angola possesses fine natural harbours and is strategically important. Before the war of liberation her economy had been booming. It enjoys largely unexploited natural resources of mineral wealth such as oil, diamonds, copper, and iron, as well as primary commodities like raw cotton, coffee beans, sisal, bananas, fish meal, and wood. It is a large country, twice the size of Texas, and only 2 per cent of its arable land is under intensive cultivation. Subsistence farming and illiteracy among its 6 million black population is common. With no obvious successor to the Portuguese, each superpower sought such a prize and its potential influence in black Africa.

Although the United States lacked a positive African policy, since Kennedy's administration it had covertly supported Holden Roberto's FNLA. Publicly neutral to all liberation movements, the United States had indulged in activities in Angola through the CIA. The United States was Angola's principal export market, and is the third largest importer to Angola. Angolan oil,

Armed by the Soviet Union. A soldier of the MPLA on guard in Luanda clutches a Soviet automatic weapon.

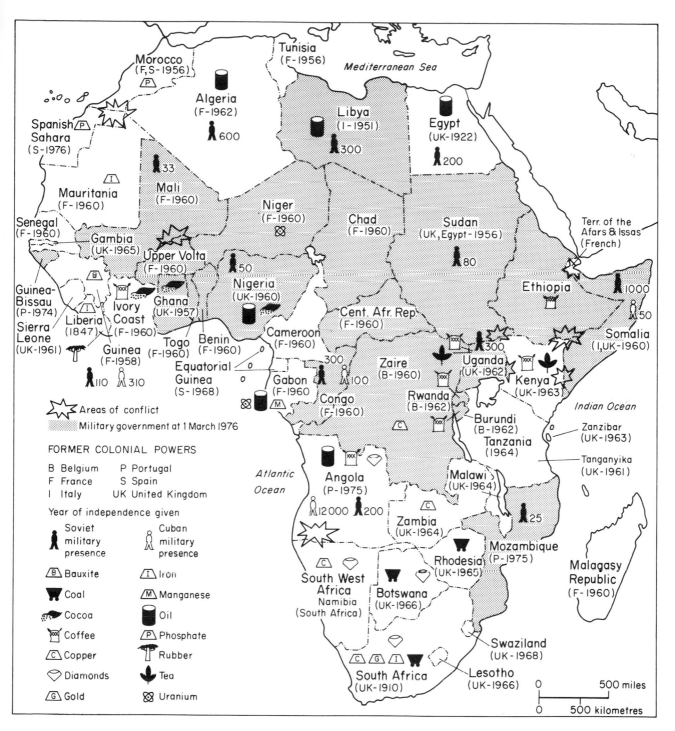

Morocco
(F,S-1956)

Tunisia
(F-1956)

Mediterranean Sea

Algeria
(F-1962)
600

Libya
(I-1951)
300

Egypt
(UK-1922)
200

Spanish
Sahara
(S-1976)

Mauritania
(F-1960)

Mali
(F-1960)
33

Niger
(F-1960)

Chad
(F-1960)

Sudan
(UK,Egypt-1956)
80

Terr. of the
Afars & Issas
(French)

Senegal
(F-1960)

Gambia
(UK-1965)

Upper Volta
(F-1960)
50

Nigeria
(UK-1960)

Cent. Afr. Rep
(F-1960)

Ethiopia
1000

Somalia
(I,UK-1960)
50

Guinea-
Bissau
(P-1974)

Sierra
Leone
(UK-1961)

Liberia
(1847)

Ivory
Coast
(F-1960)

Ghana
(UK-1957)

Togo
(F-1960)

Benin
(F-1960)

Cameroon
(F-1960)

Guinea
(F-1958)
110   310

Equatorial
Guinea
(S-1968)

Gabon
(F-1960)
300   100

Congo
(F-1960)

Zaire
(B-1960)

Uganda
(UK-1962)
300

Rwanda
(B-1962)

Kenya
(UK-1963)

Indian Ocean

Burundi
(B-1962)

Tanzania
(1964)

Zanzibar
(UK-1963)

Tanganyika
(UK-1961)

Atlantic
Ocean

Angola
(P-1975)
12 000   200

Malawi
(UK-1964)
25

Zambia
(UK-1964)

Mozambique
(P-1975)

Malagasy
Republic
(F-1960)

Rhodesia
(UK-1965)

South West
Africa
Namibia
(South Africa)

Botswana
(UK-1966)

Swaziland
(UK-1968)

Lesotho
(UK-1966)

South Africa
(UK-1910)

Areas of conflict

Military government at 1 March 1976

FORMER COLONIAL POWERS

B Belgium   P Portugal
F France   S Spain
I Italy   UK United Kingdom

Year of independence given

Soviet
military
presence

Cuban
military
presence

B Bauxite   I Iron
Coal   M Manganese
Cocoa   Oil
Coffee   P Phosphate
C Copper   Rubber
Diamonds   Tea
G Gold   Uranium

500 miles

500 kilometres

Soviet involvement in Africa in early 1976.

produced in the enclave of Cabinda in the north, provide Gulf Oil Company with 150 000 barrels a day. For a while in 1975 there was the ironic situation whereby Gulf Oil, America's fourth largest oil company, worked the oilfields, providing 500 million dollars a year to the Angolan authorities, to all intents and purposes the MPLA, whom the United States government opposed and to whom their patrons, the Soviet Union, gave considerably less than that sum! The United States suffered from several handicaps in endeavouring to intervene in Angola. For years the United States had ignored colonial mismanagement and oppression by the Portuguese because

Portugal was a NATO ally which offered useful bases. The United States had no record of helping liberation movements. It was identified with imperial Europe and still suffered from listlessness after the shock of Vietnam.

China had no economic interests in Angola but was aware of the ideological and political possibilities offered by winning influence there. Chinese leaders were sensitive to the image of small, black guerrilla units fighting one of the imperialist powers in decline. All three of the liberation movement leaders visited Peking. In 1968 Jonas Savimbi, the leader of the UNITA forces, which had broken with Roberto's FNLA in 1964, went to China and was given help, but later looked to America for support. The MPLA leader, Agostinho Neto, was welcomed in Peking, but maintained his orientation towards Moscow. In 1973 Holden Roberto returned from Peking with promises of 100 guerrilla warfare advisers and 450 tons of

Chinese military equipment. By thus aiding the most obviously 'Western' of the insurgents, China showed how ready it was to sacrifice its ideological stand for political gain, seizing the opportunity to align itself firmly against the Russians. There are considerable Chinese interests elsewhere in Africa, however, and in July 1975, when the OAU (Organization of African Unity) called upon them to observe neutrality, the Chinese immediately withdrew from FNLA bases. China was unable to match the huge Soviet aid being flown in to the MPLA, but no doubt felt sure that the United States would pre-empt any major success by the Soviet Union. Bitter propaganda between the two communist superpowers developed into a war of words:

People have become increasingly aware that in contending for hegemony with the other superpower, the Soviet revisionists stoop to anything to frenziedly penetrate and expand in Africa in a vain attempt to replace the old colonialism. Their intervention in the internal affairs of Angola constitutes an important stage in their scramble for hegemony in Africa, their aim being to place strategically important Angola, which is rich in natural resources, in their neo-colonialist spheres of influence.

Armed by China. Chinese 103mm shells captured by the MPLA. White mercenaries from the Western countries were also taken prisoner.

All the action taken by the Peking leadership shows that the Maoists, who are seeking their own hegemonic control (over the world), have not stopped subversive activity against the Angolan people for a single minute, that they gave active support to pro-imperialist groupings and organisations, pushing them to take action against the genuine representatives and vanguard of the Angolan people – the MPLA. (Colin Legum, 'The Soviet Union, China and the West in Southern Africa, *Foreign Affairs*, vol. 54, no. 4, July 1976)

Soviet backing for the MPLA was direct. They supported Dr Agostinho Neto, the founder of the Angolan Communist Party in 1956, from the first. Launching his attacks on Angola from Brazzaville in the neighbouring Congo, he proved an enterprising military leader and scored early successes. The Soviet Union endeavoured to use their influence with another African client, President Amin of Uganda, who at the time was also President of the OAU, to declare the MPLA the sole legal authority in Angola, but to no avail, since the vote was evenly matched, 22:22. President Kaunda of Zambia was moved to remark: 'Power is now in the hands of the superpowers, to whom we are handing Africa by our failure.'

From July 1975, Soviet military aid to the MPLA was all too obvious. Giant AN-22 transport planes flew in tons of weapons and equipment from the Soviet Union, including T34 tanks, AK-47 rifles, machine guns, bazookas, and rockets. Soviet MIG-21 squadrons were stationed at Brazzaville and Pointe Noire. From August, 400 Soviet technicians were known to be in the Luanda area, and on 21 Novemeber UNITA troops captured 20 Russians. During 1975 the Soviet Union poured 300 million dollars of aid into the MPLA forces. Johnny Eduardo, an FNLA leader, complained: 'Whenever Ford or Kissinger bang their fists on the table against our enemies, the Russians take them seriously and increase their military aid to the MPLA. The Americans don't match this by aid to us.'

Even so, during 1975 the United States sent 30 million dollars via neighbouring black African states to strengthen the effort against the MPLA.

Neither the Soviet Union or the United States was willing to risk a confrontation between their own troops. The United States still languished in its post-Vietnam mood of withdrawal and doubt, apprehensive of delicate foreign involvements. Neither did she employ political methods via the UN, OAU, or neutrals to forestall Soviet initiatives. The Soviet Union was thus free to orchestrate MPLA success through the proxy actions of a client communist state, Cuba. In an unexpected expedition, Cuba airlifted 12 000 troops to Angola to spearhead MPLA attacks and provide more sophisticated tactics. That Cuban troops were in action in Angola as early as August has been disputed:

The decision to send troops to Angola was taken on November 5th, 1975, at a meeting of the Cuban Communist Party. . . . The Cuban Government notified the Soviet Union of 'Operation Carlotta' after the November 5th party meeting. It was Cuba's decision to intervene and the Soviet authorities were informed afterwards. . . . The crossing took about 20 days in the face of 'provocations of all kinds from American ships and war planes'. . . . The first route had to be abandoned after American pressure on Barbados to stop Cuban aircraft re-fuelling at Bridgetown. . . . More serious was American intervention in Guyana. Initially the American oil company Texaco refused to supply fuel for Cuban aircraft landing at Georgetown. Then the US envoy there told the Guyanan Government that the airport would be bombed if the Cubans continued to land there. The Guyanans refused to give way, but as no fuel was available, the Cubans had to fly direct from . . . southern Cuba to Brazzaville, Congo, carrying extra fuel on board. (Gabriel Garcia-Marques, quoted in *The Times*, London, 11 January 1977)

By December 1975, it was clear that the FNLA-UNITA forces were losing ground. Requests from President Ford and Dr Henry Kissinger to send aid were defeated by votes in Congress. It had been hoped that if the MPLA advances could be staunched a negotiated settlement might result. Public opinion would not countenance another Vietnam, although ironically the purely military task might have been easier.

The Senate will have shown, moreover, that it — and implicitly the American people — are not being stampeded any longer into rash military ventures by cold war oratory and overblown threats of 'vast' Communist gains. The Senate was not lured into some Kissinger-style game of world power-balancing, to be played on tricky local ground, on the theory that everything the Soviets do or may do has to be matched or topped by the United States, else the rest of the world will consider Washington a 98-pound weakling . . . . It is not even clear that the MPLA . . . is 'pro-Soviet' in the sense of being Moscow's 'puppet'. (Tom Wicker, in *New York Times*, 21 December 1975)

However, in January 1976, Angola became a Marxist-Leninist republic and in October President Neto, as he now was, visited Moscow to sign a 20-year treaty with the Soviet Union. Millions of dollars' worth of arms and equipment have been provided to support the Russian and Cuban advisers and troops who are organizing, training, and garrisoning Angola, and who led further incursions into the Shaba province of neighbouring Zaire in April 1977.

President Neto is now in direct control of a programme of nationalisation and expropriation of private property, and of a foreign policy based on support for revolutionary movements throughout Africa. Russian advisers are in direct control of the Ministry of Defence, and Cuban advisers virtually monopolise the appointments on President Neto's personal staff. . . . Angola has become, for all practical purposes, a Soviet client state, and the principal base for the further development of Russia's African strategy. (Lord Chalfont, in *The Times*, London, 22 November 1976)

Guerrilla forces of UNITA still operate in the south of Angola and control large tracts of grain-producing areas in the centre of the country, effectively denying the new government the use of the key Benguela Railway. Savimbi's troops are closer than ever to the capital. Requests are constantly made for more help from the West. Fears are now expressed for the security of neighbouring black African states and for the future of Rhodesia and South Africa. Black unrest could be used to unsettle the military and economic balance by threatening the political stability and mineral wealth of these countries. The Soviet Union has proved itself willing to back such attempts and capable of keeping them supplied. Having already established important footholds on the Horn of Africa in Somalia, the Soviet Union could soon be in a position to threaten the Cape oil routes and international sea lanes as well as the interior of the African continent.

Lenin in Africa. A giant poster of the founder of the Soviet State proclaims Angola as a Marxist-Leninist state.

DISSENT IN RUSSIA

Everyone has the right to freedom of opinion and expression; this right includes freedom to hold opinions without interference and to seek, receive and impart information and ideas through any media and regardless of frontiers. (Article 19, United Nations' Universal Declaration of Human Rights)

The Soviet Union has always operated on the maxim that in unity there is strength. Freedom of opinion and expression are luxuries the superpower has not felt able to afford its citizens. Dissent, minority protest, public demonstrations have all been traditionally snuffed out. Although the Soviet Union was a signatory of the Universal Declaration of Human Rights and the Helsinki Conference on Security and Co-operation in Europe in 1975, there seem to be few such human rights within its borders or among its satellite states.

Illegal and underground press has existed in Russia since the tsars. Stalin's police and camp repression was notorious. Even Khrushchev's more liberal regime felt it prudent to suppress Pasternak's *Dr Zhivago* and Solzhenitsyn's *One Day in the Life of Ivan Denisovitch*. In February 1966, the writers Andrei Sinyavsky and Yuri Daniel received savage sentences of seven and five years' hard labour for publishing their books abroad. Public revulsion and protest in the West took on a new awareness. Even tighter control was imposed within the Soviet Union. Two secret police generals joined the Supreme Court. Soviet state power did not relish the limelight of world attention.

Apart from the concern for individual freedom and the admiration of small groups of individuals against the might of a superpower, the West was taken with the David and Goliath nature of the struggle. The story of Alexander Solzhenitsyn perhaps had greatest impact in the West. Born in 1918 in Kislovodsk six months after his father had been killed on the German front, Solzhenitsyn became a student of mathematics, history, philosophy, and literature. A major in the artillery during the Second World War, he was highly decorated. In February 1945, however, he was arrested when the censor read some disrespectful remarks he had made about Stalin in a letter to an old school-friend. He was sent to the prison camps for eight years, developing cancer while a smelter in one camp, and later he was exiled without trial to Kazakhstan, where he became a teacher. Released and rehabilitated in 1956, Solzhenitsyn began to write. *One Day in the Life of Ivan Denisovitch* was the only book he was allowed to publish in his own country. His others, *Cancer Ward*, *The First Circle*, *August 1914*, and *The Gulag Archipelago*, were all smuggled to the West for publication, and he became regarded as a literary genius as well as a courageous critic of the Soviet system's abuses. In 1967 he wrote an open letter to the Fourth Congress of Soviet Writers, speaking out against:

the now intolerable oppression of the censorship. . . . Not provided for by the Constitution, and therefore illegal, it is nowhere called by its proper name and goes under the mysterious label of Glavit . . . [because of this] survival of the Middle Ages . . . are workers not trusted, not endowed with the right to express their contrary judgements about the moral life of man and society, to interpret in their own way social problems or the historical experience which has been lived through with so much suffering in our country.

In 1970 Solzhenitsyn was awarded the Nobel Prize for literature but was prevented from delivering his acceptance speech in person. His wife gave it for him. At one point he had written: 'There are no internal affairs left on this globe of ours. And mankind can only be saved if everybody takes an interest in everybody else's affairs.' It was a *cri de coeur* for the West to maintain interest and pressure on what was happening to people like himself in Russia. It was also a reflection on how the world had shrunk and how necessary it is to adopt an international approach to our problems. He persisted in speaking out, seeking publicity and endeavouring to embarrass the Soviet Union. On 12 February 1974, he was arrested in Moscow, deprived of his citizenship, and he departed to West Germany. Since then he has travelled and lectured widely in the West and now lives in Vermont.

Solzhenitsyn was lucky; he was well known in the West and was therefore dangerous to the Soviet authorities. It would have cost them public face to make too much of an example of him. They found it easier, after bullying and threatening him, to let him go. Another leading Soviet dissident, Andrei Sakharov, knows that to leave would solve the problem for the Soviet Union. A nuclear physicist of great repute, a respected member of the Soviet Academy of Sciences, Sakharov once enjoyed considerable comfort and prestige as a hero of the Soviet Union. During the 1960s he began to criticize state policy and joined the dissident movement, founding the Committee for Human Rights in 1970. He has endured most of the usual KGB methods of intimidation: curtailment of privileges, threats on the telephone, arrests, interrogation, house searches, dismissal from work, surveillance, and physical attack. His cramped apartment in Moscow is a Mecca for Western journalists and those concerned in the dissident movement.

The problem is that in order to achieve a good life here, one necessarily develops a certain mentality. For most people, there is no opportunity to compare the system here with systems outside. The material side of life here has improved and people know it. So humans work, live and exist here, not knowing of any other kind of life. . . . Everyone wants to have a job, be married, have children, be happy, but dissidents must be prepared to see their lives destroyed and those dear to them hurt. (*Time Magazine*, 21 February 1977)

It can be argued that the present system suits the Soviet people reasonably well, bearing in mind their chequered political development and their need to concentrate on certain economic priorities before others. In such an argument, the protesters are simply the gadflies of society, products of a law which states that any social system will endanger such and such a minimum percentage of malcontents. In that case, the Soviet authorities are perfectly

right to suppress protest, and even to treat it as a form of schizophrenia. As social engineers, they are merely cleansing a few molehills which impede the construction of a pyramid. When a pyramid is built, there will be no more molehills, because all the moles will come to live in it happily ever after. (David Bonavia, *Fat Sasha and the Urban Guerrilla*, Atheneum, 1973)

Yet the molehills are there, and they seem to be getting bigger and more numerous. There may be 10 000 political prisoners in the Soviet Union. Two thousand people identified themselves by name with the Democratic Movement in 1972. There are thousands more who must read, circularize, and sympathize with the dissident press. The word 'Samizdat' (opposite to 'Gosizdat', the state publishing house) was coined in 1966. Since then Samizdat has become a forum of free thought and expression. People read type-scripts, re-type them and pass them around indefinitely. People able to travel or Western tourists often take them to the West, where several have been published or broadcast on Western radio. 'Tamizdat' is the Western press or emigré journals outside Russia. The Western radio is widely listened to in the Soviet Union and causes the authorities many problems.

It is now possible for news to be swiftly transmitted to the West and to the Third World. The Soviet Union is acutely aware that its actions can appear pilloried in the Western press and that this might permeate back into the country. They are very concerned at their international image and press coverage. Dissidents like Solzhenitsyn; Pavel Litvinov, the grandson of Stalin's Foreign Minister, who demonstrated against both the invasion of Czechoslovakia and the imprisonment of Alexander Ginsburg; the Panovs, the ballet dancers who caught the full sympathy of the West; Bukovsky, who met the President of the United States; and Dr Shtern, who was championed incessantly by Bernard Levin in *The Times* are all well-known figures who were allowed to emigrate by the authorities, who realized that the continued mistreatment of such celebrities attracted bad publicity and critical world opinion. The Soviet Union has been concerned for good relations with the West, for détente, for economic agreements. As Anatoli Shchransky said: 'World opinion is what keeps

Soviet dissident welcomed at the White House. Vladimir Bukovsky, who spent twelve of his thirty-four years in Soviet prisons for his civil rights activities, met President Carter and Vice-President Mondale, seen here with Bukovsky at the White House, in March, 1977.

us going, what keeps us alive.' Many fear that any relaxation of pressure by the authorities will in fact result in faction-fighting or disintegration by the small and disunited groups of dissidents.

Détente has brought very little in the way of results for dissidents in the Soviet Union. Brave men like Major-General Grigorenko, although pronounced sane and well by Soviet doctors, languish in psychiatric hospitals. Thousands of Russian Jews have been refused permission to emigrate. Despite the Helsinki Agreement, 3 600 fewer visas were issued in 1975 than in the previous year. Yuri Orlov, 52-year-old physicist who set up an 11-man group to monitor the Soviet Union's observation of the Helsinki Agreement, has been arrested. Personal freedom and freedom of expression seem as remote as ever. Dr Kissinger hoped to link superpower détente and arms limitations to such mutual concerns as human rights and commercial agreements. Senator Jackson put forward a proviso on the grain deals with the Soviet Union, asking: 'Fifty years ago Lenin promised the Soviet people bread and freedom. If the American farmers are to provide the bread, is it too much to ask that the Soviet leaders provide their own people a measure of freedom?'

The Soviet Union has many serious problems: the population does not have enough to eat, Soviet agriculture is obsolete, hostility between ethnic groups is increasing. The regime does not solve the problems — it merely prevents them from being raised. Every Soviet citizen from childhood is well aware that if he voices his dissatisfaction he ends up in jail. In the United States a cold winter and fuel shortage immediately become a national problem that is examined by the President and Congress. In the USSR people have not had enough food or clothing for 60 years, but their dissatisfaction concerns only the KGB. (Natalya Solzhenitsyn, in *Time Magazine*, 21 February 1977)

INDEX